Concorde

GW00775954

HISTORIC COMMERCIAL AIRCRAFT SERIES, VOLUME 10

Contents page image: Concorde 001 F-WTSS, with Aerospatiale test pilot André Turcat, Jacques Guignard as co-pilot, Michel Retief as the flight engineer and three flight test observers on board, was flown manually with the undercarriage and nose down during the 42-minute maiden flight, which ended with a perfect landing back at Toulouse at 1608hrs. (Airbus Group)

Published by Key Books
An imprint of Key Publishing Ltd
PO Box 100
Stamford
Lincs PE19 1XQ

www.keypublishing.com

Original edition published as *Aeroplane Classic Airliner: Concorde* © 2014, edited by Martyn Chorlton

This edition © 2022

ISBN 978 1 80282 375 2

Typeset by SJmagic DESIGN SERVICES, India.

Contents

Introduction

The desire for airliners that could fly faster and higher than all that had gone before them was ingrained into the commercial aviation world from the end of World War Two. While economic operation was an important factor, especially for the smaller operators, it was not at the forefront of the designers' minds when they began to pen the lines of one of the world's most amazing aircraft back in the late 1950s. As early as 1954, with the Comet programme already floundering, talks began in Britain regarding the feasibility of a Supersonic Transport (SST). This resulted, in October 1956, in the formation of the Supersonic Transport Advisory Committee (STAC), which would be in charge of development of and be responsible for the many manufacturers that would be needed to build the aircraft, named Concorde in 1963.

Six years later, the result of an incredible working partnership between the British and the French saw the first prototype take off from Toulouse on 2 March 1969, with André Turcat at the controls, while the second, British-built Concorde took off from Filton on 9 April, in the hands of British Airways Corporation (BAC) chief test pilot, Brian Trubshaw.

Although G-BOAC was destined to become the British Airways flagship, it was G-BOAA that was delivered to the airline first on 14 January 1976, after a 42-minute flight from Fairford to Heathrow. After 22,768hrs 56mins in the air, G-BOAA was retired on 12 August 2000 and today is preserved in its own hangar at the Museum of Flight, East Fortune. (Via *Aeroplane*)

With over 70 aircraft already on order, Concorde was set to be a commercial success, but as the price of oil began to rise and with the sudden realisation that the running costs of a Mach 2 airliner were considerably higher than anticipated, all except the British Overseas Aircraft Corporation (BOAC) and Air France fell by the wayside. Like so many projects before it, this should have brought the entire concept to a shuddering halt, but both the British and French governments had invested heavily, and there was too much to lose by scrapping the aircraft. In the end, just 20 aircraft were built, six of them were the prototypes, development and pre-production aircraft, and just seven aircraft apiece were destined to be operated by the new British Airways (BA) and Air France.

Even in service, Concorde struggled to be accepted in many countries, especially the US, where the noise of the Olympus engines was always the main sticking point, although, even at Heathrow, many protests failed to stop BA basing its main fleet there. Bearing in mind the complexity of the aircraft, it was one of the world's safest, considering the distances it travelled and the eye-watering speed at which it flew. This made the loss of the Air France Concorde in 2000 a particularly unfitting 'beginning of the end' for the airliner, which courted controversy right to the finale. It was a combination of factors that saw the airliner enter retirement three years later, but the bottom line was that Concorde was getting old, and, despite being built like the proverbial 'brick outhouse', constant supersonic cycles take their toll, and that kind of punishment would not be expected of a military aircraft, let alone a civilian one.

There was never any hope of recovering the £1.3bn that had been invested in the development programme, and only BA managed to turn a profit during the 1980s and early 1990s. However, setting aside the economics, Concorde was an incredible achievement from the outset, built by two different nations, which overcame every technical problem that arose (which were innumerable) to produce, by far, the most iconic airliner ever built.

Brian Trubshaw brings Concorde 002 into land at Fairford on its maiden flight on 9 April 1969, without the aid of both radio altimeters. (Via François Prins)

Chapter 1

The Supersonic Transport (SST) Story

Pushing the envelope

Britain was no stranger to supersonic flight; the first home-grown aircraft to breach the speed of sound was the DH.108 on 9 September 1948. However, Britain should have been the first because, back in 1943, a specification was issued for an experimental aircraft that was capable of reaching Mach 1.5 at 36,500ft. The aircraft, the Miles M.52, had the potential for this eye-watering speed and more, but, in typical British fashion, the project was cancelled in February 1946 as a result of some very deep cuts by the new Labour government. However, it was no coincidence that, across the Atlantic, the Bell XS-1 (aka X-1), which bore an uncanny resemblance to the M.52, had just made its maiden flight, albeit the first of several glide flights, before further testing under its own power. When cancelled, the first of three M.52s under construction was more than 80 per cent complete, and, with an intensive flight test programme planned by the Royal Aircraft Establishment (RAE), it was confidently predicted that Mach 1 would be achieved before 1946 was over.

Other reasons for cancelling the M.52 included pilot safety, and that the aircraft's straight wing, adopted by the Bell X-1, was not the way forward with supersonic flight; captured German research with swept wing technology was. The latter, in particular, would prove correct, but this did not take away from the fact that the US was handed the prize of breaching the speed of sound first, while Britain had to settle for achieving the same with an unmanned radio-controlled version of the M.52, air launched from a Mosquito. Still a great achievement in its own right, the 30 per cent scale M.52 reached Mach 1.38 in level flight on 10 October 1948, before contact was lost and the Armstrong Siddeley Beta-powered model disappeared out into the Atlantic. Only days later, again across the Atlantic, the XP-86 Sabre became the first production fighter to break Mach 1 in a dive, and, on 27 May 1953, the YF-100 Super Sabre broke the magic number in level flight on its first outing. The record breaking seemed to be confined to the US until, finally, on 10 October 1956, Peter Twiss in the Fairey FD.2 captured the world air speed for Britain at Mach 1.73 (1,132mph); a record that was destined to remain in British hands for over a year. Although not a production aircraft, the FD.2, which was also the world's first aircraft to exceed 1,000mph, would prove to be an exceptionally useful test vehicle for the future of the SST and, once modified as the BAC 221, would prove invaluable in testing the design of Concorde's wing many years later.

In 1954, a team led by Dr Dietrich Küchemann decided to design their own supersonic airliner based on the Avro 740 bomber. The aircraft was redesigned with a 72-seat capacity and a cruising speed of Mach 2.5. To cope with the speed, the fuselage would have to be made of stainless steel and, to test the theory, Bristol was contracted to build the Type 188. The research gleaned from this project was expected to be used to support several subsonic jet airliner projects, including the promising Vickers V.1000. However, the V.1000 was cancelled on 29 November 1955, owing to a lack of interest from BOAC, which then rubbed salt into the wound by ordering a fleet of American-built Boeing 707s. It was time for the British aircraft industry to try something radical.

One of the great aviation icons of the 20th century, Concorde was developed and built by British and French engineers. (Martyn Chorlton)

The Bristol (later British Aircraft Corporation [BAC])-designed Type 198 had all the ingredients of the future Concorde from the start. With a proposed take-off weight of 385,000lb and power from six Olympus engines, the Type 198 was described as 'too ambitious'. (Martyn Chorlton)

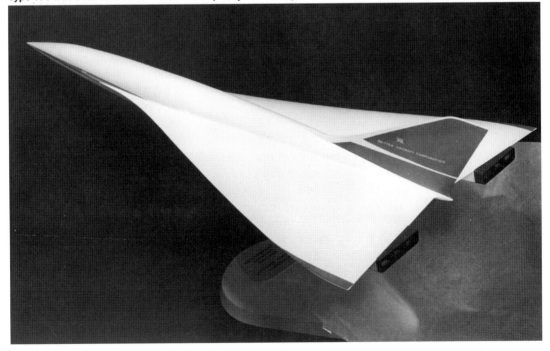

STAC

There was no doubt that the airline industry, from the outset, was looking for faster airliners. Britain was at the forefront of this quest during the post-war period, beginning with the de Havilland Comet, which first flew in July 1949. It was such a shame that this great aircraft missed out by a hair's breadth of becoming the first-generation jetliner for the world's airlines, as it would have undoubtedly laid the foundations for the next generation. By the mid-1950s, just as the Comet programme began to falter, talks began between the Controller of Aircraft, M. B. Morgan (later Sir Morien), and the leaders of all of Britain's aircraft manufacturers to discuss the feasibility of producing a supersonic airliner. For a more cohesive response, a committee was formed under the name STAC on 1 October 1956, with Morgan as the chairman.

STAC gathered together all of the best aviation brains in country, representatives from engine and airframe manufacturers, government technologists and individuals from various airlines. At this point, no one could have predicted the amount of opposition that the aircraft would create and the obstacles that would be put in its way by countries such as the US, let alone that the cost of fuel would soar through the roof just as the aircraft was being prepared to enter service. The only problems that could be predicted were technical, and, although they could be overcome the SST would present hurdles of its own, which were much higher than those placed by a normal airliner.

A wind tunnel model of the Armstrong Whitworth proposal for a supersonic transport (SST) with an 'M' planform wing. This wing configuration had the advantage of not causing sonic booms at ground level. (Martyn Chorlton)

Design concepts

There was no doubting from the start that the design of any supersonic airliner would involve the novel configuration of a long, thin body with the smallest cross-section possible and a low aspect ratio wing. STAC reduced the number of proposals down to three conceivable designs. The first was the most unusual and was presented by Armstrong Whitworth: an airliner with an 'M-wing' layout, which swept forward from the wing root and then back towards the wing tips. This design was capable of cruising at Mach 1.2 (800mph) with a range of 1,500 miles. The second was designed to cruise at Mach 1.8, fly for up to 3,500 miles and was very similar to the final layout. The last design was the huge Handley Page HP.109, powered by eight engines made of steel and titanium, with a potential cruising speed of Mach 3. The latter was ruled out at a very early stage due to being far too costly to develop, but, in the US, a very similar design appeared as the XB-70 Valkyrie bomber, and further development as an airliner continued for many years after but never reached the prototype stage.

By early 1959, and after studying all three designs, STAC tightened the criteria by recommending that the new SST should be capable of Mach 1.2 for short-range operations and Mach 1.8 on transatlantic routes. The Ministry of Aviation (MoA) issued contracts for more detailed studies that would reveal, by late 1960, that a slim delta configuration with an ogee (curved) leading edge was the most aerodynamic design, which was good for Mach 2.2. This increased cruising speed was good news for reducing journey times.

Just before the famous name of Bristol was being merged into the new British Aircraft Corporation (BAC), the company had been working on a promising layout designated as the Type 198 and designed by a team led by Bill Strang, Mick Wilde, Doug Thorn and Douglas Vickery, all overseen by Chief Designer Archibald 'Doc' Russell (later Sir Archibald). Very similar in appearance to the future Concorde, the aircraft could carry 130 passengers, had a take-off weight of 385,000lb and power was provided by six Olympus turbojets, each rated at 25,000lb thrust. The MoA thought that the Type 198 was a little ambitious, but, rather than dismissing it out of hand, it asked the Bristol designers to produce a 100-passenger version, powered by four Olympus engines and with a reduced take-off weight of 250,000lb. Despite protests, Russell and his team returned to the drawing board and produced the smaller Type 233 (BAC 223).

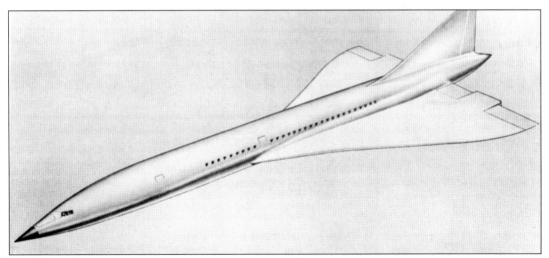

Looking every inch a winner, it was by the hands of Bristol designers that the Type 223 was penned. Within a decade, the result, Concorde, would be lifting from Filton's runway. (Martyn Chorlton)

Concorde

Sir Archibald Russell was an engineer who spent the majority of his career with Bristol, and, once the company merged with BAC, he became managing director of the Filton Division. Russell was joint chairman of the Concorde Executive Committee of Directors from 1965 to 1969. (Martyn Chorlton)

TECHNICAL DATA – BRISTOL/BAC TYPE 198 & 223

ENGINES: (198) Six 22,800lb Olympus Mk 591; (223) four 28,000lb Olympus Mk 593
WINGSPAN: (198) 78ft; (223) 70ft
LENGTH: (198) 180ft; (223) 176ft 6in
HEIGHT: (198) 40ft 4in; (223) 35ft
MAX SPEED: (198) 1,400mph; (223)1,450mph
RANGE: (198) 3,600 miles; (223) 3,300 miles
LOADED WEIGHT: (198) 385,000lb; (223) 251,700lb
ACCOMMODATION: (198) Six crew and 122 passengers; (223) Six crew and 90 passengers

10

Singing from a similar hymn sheet!

Across the Channel, Air France issued a study contract to Sud Aviation in 1957, while in Britain, the nation's flag carrier, BOAC, was not interested in SSTs. The Air France request was for an aircraft that could carry the same passenger numbers as the Caravelle (80) over a distance of 2,000 miles but at Mach 2. Led by Pierre Sartre and Lucien Servantry, the French design worked closely with Dassault, which was already carrying out Mach 2 testing using the same delta wing as its successful Mirage fighter. As a result, the French came up with virtually the same conclusion as the British; the ogee wing shape was the only way forward.

At the same time, at the insistence of the British government, the Ministry of Supply (MoS) was ordered to look for foreign partners to share the exorbitant cost of the SST. Sud Aviation was the only positive response received, and, on 12 June 1959, Aubrey Jones of the MoS went to that year's Paris Air Salon and handed over the STAC findings to the French. In June 1961, Sud Aviation, which was on the verge of becoming Aérospatiale, displayed a model of its SST, which it named the Super Caravelle.

The similarity, on the surface, between the British Type 223 and the French Super Caravelle was uncanny; although the size, weight and range differed, the only major difference was that Sud did not fit a hinged nose, which BAC, quite rightly, considered to be an essential feature because of the high

An engineer carries out a few final touches to an impressive wooden wind-tunnel model of a Concorde at Royal Aircraft Establishment (RAE) Bedford on 9 February 1968. (Martyn Chorlton)

Built purely to carry out low-speed test flying as part of the development programme, the HP.115 was no looker, but it handled well and was a major asset to the project until it was retired in 1974. Today, the aircraft is preserved alongside Concorde G-BSST and the BAC 221 at the Fleet Air Arm Museum. (Martyn Chorlton)

angle of the nose during landing. Both British and French governments agreed that it would be wrong to develop two separate aircraft that shared so much in common, and both BAC and Sud Aviation were instructed to collaborate. After many meetings, a Franco-British agreement was signed on 29 November 1962 by General André Puget and Sir George Edwards.

The two governments agreed to split the costs of the project 50/50, with the main construction of the airframe being shared between BAC and Aérospatiale, while Bristol Siddeley (Rolls-Royce from 1966) and SNECMA (Société Nationale d'Ètude et de Construction de Moteurs d'Aviation) would jointly work on the engines. Two versions of the aircraft were to be produced: a transatlantic variant by the British partner and a short-haul model by the French, complete with a ventral stairway instead of a fuel tank in the rear fuselage. Both the airframe and engine production were overseen by a committee of directors and each nation's industrial group was contracted by their respective governments.

Multi-national talent

Anglo-French projects would follow in the future, but they would never be on a par with the amount of collaboration and, ultimately, goodwill that was needed to create such a technically challenging aircraft. It took strong leadership to keep the programme on track, and only a man such as Sir George Edwards, who was the architect of the entire project, could carry it off. From the senior designers through to the engineers building the airframe and engines, to the innumerable suppliers of systems and equipment, collaboration was the key to success and this would be achieved.

While the French had set out to design their short-haul variant, they had to concede that the transatlantic SST was the way forward, especially after feedback from several potential airline customers in 1963. Many airlines did not think that the ideas presented by BAC and Aérospatiale were forward thinking enough and a strong body of opinion at the time thought that the European SST would be eclipsed by the Mach 3 American SST, capable of carrying 250 passengers, in a few years' time. It was a very wise decision to keep the aircraft at the original figures of 100 passengers at Mach 2; the American SST was destined to cost the US taxpayer US$2bn with nothing to show for it.

The aircraft was officially name Concorde in 1963, by which time the design had been pushed and pulled a little more, which increased the weight from 262,000lb to 286,000lb. The passenger seating was also increased from 90 to 100 at full range, but once the Olympus engine was redesigned to the more powerful Mk 593B, the weight grew again to 326,000lb with room for up to 118 passengers. The design was finally set in stone in early 1965, enabling construction of the prototype Concordes, 001 in France and 002 in Britain, to begin in April.

A project as big as Concorde required an equally large and expensive research programme, which involved two live aircraft and a complete test airframe that was put through the simulated rigours of thousands of supersonic cycles at the RAE Farnborough. To flight test the low-speed handling characteristics of Concorde's wing, Handley Page was contracted to build the sole HP.115 research aircraft. Built at Radlett, the aircraft, serialled XP841, was first flown by J. M. Henderson from RAE Bedford on 17 August 1961. The HP.115 was an excellent aircraft that gave the Concorde engineers a colossal amount of useful information until it was retired in 1974. The second research machine was first flown as the Fairey FD.2 on 6 October 1954. The FD.2 had already carried out a great deal of supersonic study, especially on the effects of sonic booms. The aircraft would support the Concorde programme directly when it was fitted with an ogee wing and redesignated as the BAC 221 in 1961. As with the HP.115, a great deal of information was gleaned from an ogee wing in flight, and the BAC 221 continued its busy research regime until 1973.

Originally built as the Fairey F.D.2, WG774 was redesigned at Filton by Bristol engineers and renamed the BAC (aka Bristol) 221. First flown in 1964, the 221 was used for Concorde development until 1973 and, today, is preserved in the Fleet Air Arm Museum. (Martyn Chorlton)

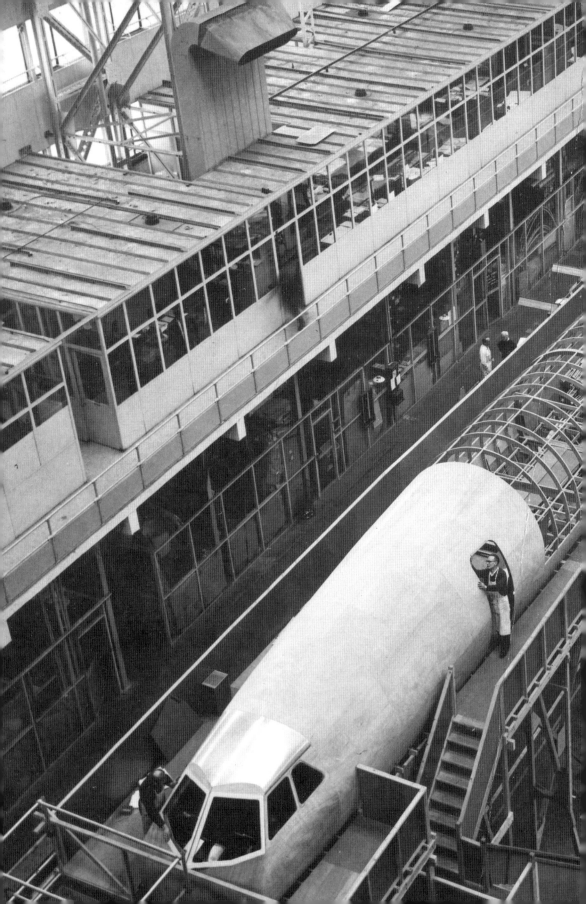

A full-scale wooden mock-up of Concorde at Filton in 1965, which proved to be invaluable during the design and manufacturing process. (Martyn Chorlton)

Chapter 2
Built for Mach 2

Shape and materials

The construction of the world's first supersonic transport can be broken down into two parts: shape and materials. As stated, the shape came out as a tailless delta with an ogee planform. This meant that, instead of the wing having two spars, all parallel to the transverse axis and increasing in length from zero, at the leading-edge root, to the full span at the rear spar, which carried the trailing-edge elevons. The wings were completed by axial fore/aft members and finally machined integrally stiffened skin panels.

The biggest units, forming the heart of the aircraft, were the five sections of integral fuselage and wing made by Aérospatiale, the rear most at Nantes, then two at Toulouse, then one at Bougenais and finally the forward section at Marignane near Marseilles. The latter had the sharply swept front sections of wing (made at Bougenais) added on each side, loads from these being transmitted through the fuselage frames. The main structure was then completed by adding the forward fuselage (measured from front to rear, the longest section of all) made by BAC at Weybridge, plus the nose sections, made by BAC at Hurn and by Marshall of Cambridge, and the long tapering rear fuselage and integral vertical tail, made at Weybridge.

Slender-delta aircraft take off and land at a high angle of attack, and, in the Fairey FD.2, the pilot had been given forward vision by arranging for the entire nose to hinge downwards. In the Concorde, this was taken further, with the solution of a hydraulically powered visor, which in cruising flight slid to the rear and upwards to give a perfect exterior profile. The initial answer was to use an opaque metal visor, giving the pilot no forward view whatsoever in cruising flight. Test pilot John Cochrane said it was 'like flying inside a letterbox'. This arrangement was rejected by the Federal Aviation Administration (FAA) in the US, in one of that organisation's justifiably critical inputs. Thus, glass that remained strong at 120°C was urgently developed, making a fully glazed retracting visor possible, which made the cockpit uncannily quiet at Mach 2 and, additionally, looked better.

The engine nacelles were attached beneath the wings and were made by BAC at Filton. Each nacelle was a rectangular box with sharp-lipped steel leading edges at the open front. Special provisions had to be made to fasten the exceedingly rigid engine inside each 40ft nacelle; they flexed with the movements of the wing, which had a thickness only 2–15 per cent of the chord. The wing spars were continuous across the top, but the wing structure left room between them for several large auxiliary units, such as the fuel-cooled heat exchangers that served the air-conditioning, lubrication and hydraulic systems.

Most of the airframe was made from an aluminium alloy called RR.58, developed by Rolls-Royce in 1928 for aero-engine pistons. For Concorde, High Duty Alloys developed it as sheet and plate, and licensed it to its French partner with the designation AU2GN. An enormous research programme was needed to certify the entire structure with local temperatures up to 127°C, as are reached in supersonic cruise. It was to alleviate thermal stress that the cruise Mach number was eventually reduced to 2, instead of the original 2.15.

For the same reason, prolonged research was needed with other materials. The hydraulic system was filled with a fluid called Oronite, kept cool by circulation through heat exchangers, though the system pressure of 4,000lb/in had been pioneered in the Bristol Britannia. This system, together with flight control, electronics and air-conditioning, was the responsibility of Aérospatiale, which tended to assign items to French or American suppliers. The pressure differential in the cabin in cruising flight was higher than in other aircraft at 10.7lb/in.

Other systems were assigned to BAC, including the complicated fuel system. The main integral tankage, tank No. 1 to No. 8, filled the entire interior of the wings. Right at the front of the wing were tanks Nos. 9 and 10, each extending across from one leading edge to the other, and behind the trailing edge was tank No. 11. At take-off, tank No. 11 was empty, but fuel was transferred to it during transonic acceleration. In the prototypes, the system capacity was 21,890 gallons, but this was increased in the production aircraft to an eventual 26,330 gallons.

The autopilot was originally an Elliott-Automation system, derived from that of the Vickers VC10 but refined by what became Marconi-Elliott. Likewise, the flight-control power units were derived from the VC10's Boulton Paul products but further developed by what had become Dowty Boulton Paul. The six elevons were each driven by an electrically signalled power unit with inbuilt artificial feel. The high hydraulic pressure enabled the power units to be remarkably small, but they still needed underwing fairings, and years were spent refining the 'fly-by-wire' system and control logic. The vertical tail included two rudders, whose power units were placed on opposite sides of the fin to make the modest

Concorde 001 F-WTSS as it was first rolled out of its hangar in front of 1,100 guests at Toulouse on 11 December 1967. (Leslie Davis via *Aeroplane*)

side-thrust of the fairings cancel out. The wing leading edge was fixed but cambered gracefully down, the curvature increasing towards the tips. Ahead of the engines, the leading edge incorporated Napier Spraymat electro-thermal de-icers.

The use of large underwing engine nacelles could have caused problems with the undercarriage, but there was sufficient room for the main gears to retract inwards. The legs were fitted between the two largest tanks, with the four-wheel bogies under the cabin floor. Each main unit was a product of Hispano-Suiza at Colombiés in southern France and the only problem was that, to make it fit inside the wing, the tyre pressure had to be 187lb/in. Tyres of special multi-ply design were provided by Kleber- Colombiés for French aircraft, and by Dunlop for the British. The tall, forward-retracting nose unit had twin wheels with hydraulic steering and was supplied by Messier (later Messier-Hispano) at Montrouge. The Dunlop disc brakes had SNECMA (Hispano) SPAD skid-control, which was vital for such a heavy and fast-landing aircraft with no flaps, airbrakes or braking parachute.

Arguably, the most remarkable thing about the Concorde story is that a production aircraft finally emerged. After repeated redesign for greater weights and engine power, at all times in a politically charged arena, almost everything had to be done at least twice to satisfy the two industries and two governments.

The British Concorde test airframe pictured at RAE Farnborough in 1973. A certification requirement of 6,800 cycles was reached by late 1975, and subsequent testing was carried out at a rate of 7,000 cycles per year (three times the rate of most 'fatigued' aircraft). (Martyn Chorlton)

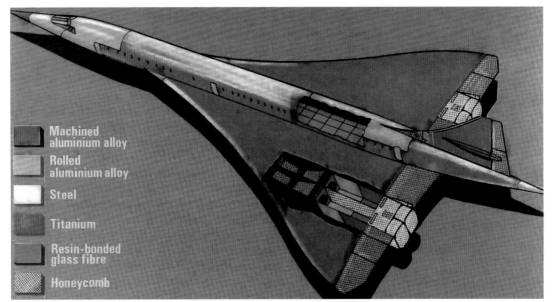

Machined
aluminium alloy

Rolled
aluminium alloy

Steel

Titanium

Resin-bonded
glass fibre

Honeycomb

A basic, but effective, diagram of the number of materials used in the construction of Concordes and their locations. (Martyn Chorlton)

Propulsion

By the time Concorde had been designed, it had been belatedly realised that, for most jet aircraft, the turbofan engine is much quieter and more fuel-efficient that the noisy, fuel-hungry turbojet. Unfortunately, fundamental questions of propulsion efficiency mean that is impossible to use the jet from a turbofan, moving at about 950mph, to propel an aircraft at Mach 2. An SST engine must generate a propulsive jet moving at some 2,000mph, and this inevitably means a lot of noise.

Engines traditionally take longer to develop than aircraft and it was fortunate that, from the outset, the Bristol Olympus was considered almost ideal. Designed in 1947–49 by Bristol's Engine Division, it became a product of Bristol Aero Engines (1959) and Rolls-Royce (1966). Originally produced at 11,000lb thrust for the Avro Vulcan bomber, it was soon developed for the Vulcan B.2 at 20,000lb, which was an astonishing achievement.

The Olympus was a pioneering two-spool engine with two axial compressors in tandem, each driven by its own turbine to give a high pressure ratio and thus good fuel economy. Later versions had new compressors handling much greater airflow, and, in 1959, a large afterburner with a variable nozzle was added to provide up to 32,610lb thrust for the BAC TSR.2 supersonic bomber. For Concorde, the basic engine was enlarged further as the Mk 593, with the afterburner and variable nozzle assigned to the French partner SNECMA, to result in what was to be a 60/40 split.

The propulsion of an SST is unlike that of subsonic aircraft. Even the TSR.2 engine merely added a big afterburner for a dash at Mach 2, burning fuel voraciously, whereas for the SST that is the cruising speed. Accordingly, most of the Mk 593 thrust had to come from the engine itself. But it is not as simple as that. At Concorde cruising speed, one gets an unusual distribution of the various forces: from the variable inlet ramp, -12 per cent (minus figure = drag); from the air-intake system, +75 per cent; from the engine, +8 per cent; and from the convergent/divergent nozzle, +29 per cent. In other words, at Mach 2 virtually all the thrust comes from the inlet (not part of the engine at all) and nozzle; the engine just keeps the flow going. It is not easy to measure the thrust and drag of each element.

As they were crucial in propelling the aircraft, the inlet and nozzle consumed at least as much design time as the basic Mk 593 engine. Whereas most of the early SST studies had a row of engines in a tight group at the back, by the time the Super Caravelle and Concorde were schemed, the best arrangement was considered to be a pair of engines under each wing. Each twin-engine nacelle was placed well outboard but not so far out as to make it difficult for the wing underside to guide the flow into the inlet at high angles of attack. Because of the need for complicated inlet and exhaust systems, the nacelles were 40ft long.

Individual nacelles were studied, but, although it increased the likelihood of trouble with one engine affecting its neighbour, the best answer would be two engines per nacelle (in the Bristol 198 each nacelle would have housed three). Creating a propulsion system that could operate reliably with the incredibly finetuning needed for maximum cruise efficiency was an excellent result and had never been achieved previously.

A basic problem was that, at Mach 2.2, the pressure in the combustion chamber was about 80 times that of the air entering the inlet. The slightest disturbance to the flow could trigger a surge (the Americans call this phenomenon an 'inlet unstart'). The high-pressure air in the combustion chamber violently reverses direction and escapes through the compressor and out of the inlet. Concorde test pilot Brian Trubshaw recalled such an event as, 'A bloody great row, smoke on the flight deck, sounds like the next war has started'. When the phenomenon was first encountered it caused structural damage to No. 4 engine of Concorde 001. Painstaking work tamed it, and later, one Olympus 593 was deliberately surged about 800 times and kept running. It was a huge achievement to make such a terrifying event almost unknown in airline service.

The answer was in the careful design of the five large movable sections of the inlet duct and nacelle. The largest was about 40in wide and 10ft long, so a pressure wave of 50lb/in puts a sudden load on that relatively flimsy panel of over 100 tons. Yet each panel had to be precisely positioned to control the enormous airflow and the exact positions of the various shockwaves.

In parallel with nacelle development, the British partner developed the engine. The Olympus 593D, rated at 32,500lb thrust, first ran in July 1964, and began flight testing in a Concorde half-nacelle attached under a Vulcan test bed in September 1966. By this time, it was clear that more thrust was needed, and eventually the 593D Mk 610 engine was certificated in April 1975 at a dry thrust of 31,350lb, boosted by the modest afterburner to 38,050lb. Stanley Hooker commented that, in cruising flight at 50,000ft, each engine gave some 10,000lb, 'but as at this speed each pound of thrust is equivalent to 4hp, the Concorde's engines are developing 160,000hp'.

The last big engine modification was to redesign the nozzle. Aérospatiale masterminded the thrust-reverser aft (TRA), which completely replaced the complex original nozzle system by relatively simple upper and lower hinged half-shells, with notched inner walls, made of precision-welded Stresskin. On afterburning take-off, these squeezed the jet and made it splay out sideways, considerably reducing noise. In flight, they were computer-programmed to optimise propulsive efficiency, and on landing they rotated like clam shells to reverse thrust.

Sadly, it is outside the scope of this work to describe all the technical breakthroughs in Concorde propulsion, but perhaps the greatest was the control system for the engine and all the variable portions of inlet and nozzle. Moreover, the prime contractor, Ultra Electronics, based this system on the first full-authority electronic engine control to be certificated for regular use. It was distantly derived from the Ultra analogue system used on the Britannia but was more automated. Later, a Concorde was flown with digital control. The afterburner was a French responsibility; so, its control system was assigned to Elecma. This was another example of duplication on political grounds, though this is in no way is a criticism of Elecma, a division of SNECMA, which did a good job. It was just another example of costly duplication on political grounds, and posterity is to consider the Concorde management structure an exercise in how not to do it.

The Hispano-designed and -built nose landing gear was positioned 40ft aft of the tip of Concorde's nose. (Martyn Chorlton)

The BAC-built forward fuselage sections of Concordes 205 to 210 are nearing completion at Weybridge. Aircraft 205 to 210 would become F-BVFA, G-BOAA, F-BVFB, G-BOAB, F-BVFC and G-BOAD, respectively. (Martyn Chorlton)

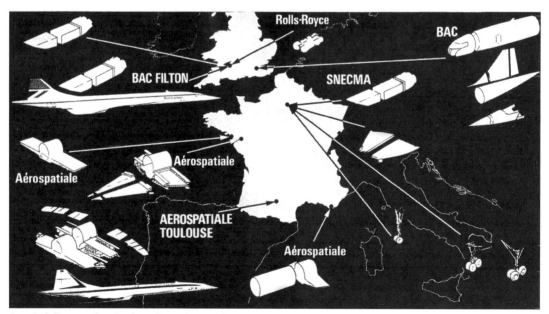

A period diagram showing how the various major components were shared between Britain and France; many subcontractors, which produced much smaller but equally important parts for Concorde, were spread much further afield. (Martyn Chorlton)

PRODUCTION – CONCORDE MAIN MANUFACTURERS AND SUBCONTRACTORS

Major components

Aérospatiale – Forward wing, centre wing, elevons (Aérospatiale Suresnes, Bouguenais) and frame 46–54 of intermediate fuselage (Bouguenais); Frame 41–46 of centre wing (Marignane); Frames 54–66 of centre wing/fuselage (Toulouse); Frame 66–72 of centre wing (St Nazaire); and outer wings (Dassault, Boulogne/Seine)

BAC – Air intakes (Preston); Engine bay (Filton); Droop nose (Hurn); Nose, forward and rear fuselage (Weybridge); and fin and rudder (Weybridge)

Hispano – Main landing gear

Messier – Nose landing gear

SNECMA – TRA nozzles

Rolls-Royce (1971) Ltd – engines

Systems

Aérospatiale – Hydraulics, flying controls, navigation, radio and air conditioning supply

BAC – Electrics, oxygen, fuel, engine instrumentation, engine controls, fire, air conditioning distribution and de-icing

British systems sub-contractors

Avica (piping and ducting systems and components); Boulton Paul (flight servo controls and amplifiers); Dowty Electrics (micro-contacts for electro-hydraulic circuits); Dowty-Rotol (electro-hydraulic selector for the landing gear and hydraulic accumulator); Dunlop (brakes and wheels); Elliott and Smiths Industries (fuel-flow meters and electronic work); English Electric (constant speed drive, electrical load control, 'Spraymat' de-icer, plastic visor and panel lighting); Flight Refuelling (refuelling equipment); Graviner (fire extinguishers and detection system); Hawker Siddeley (air conditioning); Hymatic Engineering (pressurisation of fuel tanks); Integral (hydraulic pumps); Marshall (nose and visor); Normalair (cabin pressure regulator); Page (electrical instruments and fire alarm system); Palmer (fuel filters); Plessey (fuel electro pumps, electric actuators & gas turbine starters); PPG Aerospace (paint); Rotax (contactors and de-icing electronic timer); Saunders (fuel electro valves); Smiths (icing detection); Walter Kidde (oxygen equipment)

British communications and navigation systems sub-contractors

Decca (Omnitrac equipment); EKCO (weather radar); Elliott (autopilot, flight and take-off director computers and landing display); Ferranti (inertial navigation system and automatic chart display); Kollsmann (flight instruments); Marconi (Doppler, DME and Selcal); Smiths (Navigation and engine instruments); White & Nunn (VOR/DME/ATC remote control)

French systems sub-contractors

Air Equipment/DBA (servo control automatic selectors, artificial fuel system, HP fuel pumps and control surface position indicators); Auxilec (alternators and transformers rectifiers); Bronzavia (air conditioning, HP fuel pumps, water separator and humidifier); CEM (high temperature micro-contacts); ECE (control boxes, breakers, relays and control panels); EROS (pilot's individual oxygen equipment [Prototype trials]); Intertechnique (fuel gauging and transfer systems); Jaeger (engine monitoring system and miscellaneous instruments); SAFT (accumulator battery); SECAN (hydraulic oil/fuel heat exchangers); SEMCA (air starter, pressure reducer, thermostatic valve, non-return valves, cut-off valves, drains and high temp couplings); Sofrance (hydraulic filters); Teleflex-Syneravia (landing lamps); Zenith (refuelling collector)

French communications and navigation systems sub-contractors
Crouzet (air data computer); CSF (VOR/ILS receiver); ECE (control boxes and panels); Sadelec-Wilcox (France/US) (ATC transponder and VHF communications); Sagem (inertial navigation system and navigation computer); SFENA (flight director gyro horizon and VOR-NAV indicator); SFIM (attitude indicator and oxygen regulator); Staec (antennae [ATC-DME – MARKER]); TEAM (public address system); TRT (auto-landing radio altimeter)

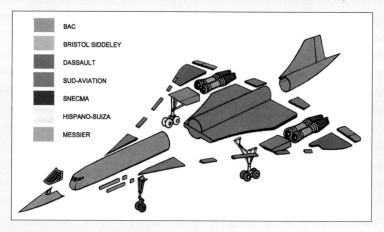

The office of Concorde, which looks particularly roomy thanks to the shot being taken with a wide-angle lens; it was, however, quite small because at this point the forward fuselage was already tapering towards the nose. The engineer's panel is to the right is broken down into individual panels, in which they can control pressurisation, air bleed, air conditioning, electrics, engines, engine in-takes, engine starts, fuel and the centre of gravity. (*Aeroplane*)

Chapter 3

Concorde – Olympus Power

'Father of the Olympus'

Stanley (later Sir) Hooker was an exceptional engineer and started work with Rolls-Royce at Derby with the challenge of increasing the power output of the Merlin. Hooker led a team of equally skilled engineers, who took the 1,000hp engine and developed it to over 2,000hp by the end of World War Two; they also developed another existing engine design into the powerful Griffon that was still operational with the Royal Air Force (RAF) in 1988. Hooker, therefore, knew what he was doing, but, unfortunately, a difference of opinion about the importance of gas turbines between him and Rolls-Royce Managing Director Ernest (later Lord) Hives did not help matters. Furthermore, Hooker had also been promised the job of chief engineer at Rolls-Royce with total responsibility for the emerging jet engine technology, but this had not happened, and Hooker left Rolls-Royce in late 1949 to join the Bristol Aircraft Company's engine department. It was to be a fortuitous move.

Gas turbine engines were still in their early stages of development in 1949, although they were far more advanced than they would have been had there not been a war to speed progress. When Hooker arrived, two of Bristol's engineers, Alec Henstridge and Sam Blackman, had already designed the world's first two-spool axial turbojet (that is two compressors each driven by its own turbine, LP and HP), which, as the BE 10, had been approved by the Bristol board and passed to the Design Department for working drawings to be made. Dr Hooker was appointed chief engineer for the engine division at Bristol in early 1950. At the time, Hooker probably knew more about gas turbines than any other engineer in the world, so it was natural that his opinion on the BE 10 (later Olympus) was sought. Hooker recalled:

> The engine was important as it had been selected by the RAF to power the Avro Vulcan, which was then being designed and built at Woodford, although the first prototype flew with Rolls-Royce Avons. I looked at the Olympus drawings and was impressed by what they had achieved. If Bristol could build this engine it would, in a single leap, make them equal with Rolls-Royce. There were many things about the engine that I did not like but overall it was sound and I knew we could make a great engine. Work on the prototypes was sanctioned and we had the first ready for test by May 1950.

Tests were successful, and the Olympus went into production for the RAF. Hooker and the team continued to develop the engine for new applications, which, apart from aircraft, included powering naval vessels and being used in power stations to generate electricity.

While Hooker was in overall charge of the programme – he was sometimes known as the 'father of the Olympus' – others were given specific tasks to carry out with the progress of the design. As the engine was installed in the Vulcan, more power was demanded from it and Pierre Young was given responsibility for the future of the Olympus. Pierre Young was an excellent choice, as, apart from being a gifted engineer, his mother was French, and he had been brought up in France to speak the language

Over 150,000lb of thrust is unleashed as a Concorde tucks away its gear during take-off. Power was reduced to a mere 40,000lb in the cruise, which equated to 17 miles to the gallon per passenger! (Via Martyn Chorlton)

as a native. This was immensely useful when it came to discussions between the two partners. Hooker has given Young the credit for getting Concorde from the drawing board to reality as, quite apart from his engineering background, he was also skilled at calming situations when matters became problematical between Britain and France.

As the engine increased in power, it was selected for other aircraft, notably for the English Electric TSR.2 multi-role aircraft. The Olympus was ideal for this remarkable aeroplane, and when it flew, it became more than apparent just how efficient the engine was. However, even before the TSR.2 had flown, the Olympus was in a strong position to be selected to power the proposed SST that had been under consideration in Britain from the mid-1950s. In France, SNECMA had been working on an engine for France's SST, the Super Caravelle, but it was not as advanced as the Olympus.

Powering the SST

At the time when the two independent SST programmes commenced, there was already a good working relationship

One of Britain's greatest engineers, Sir Stanley Hooker, joined Rolls-Royce in 1938 but, in 1949, moved on to Bristol, where he became heavily involved in the development of the Olympus. After retiring in 1970, Hooker rejoined Rolls-Royce as a technical director, retiring for second time in 1978. Sir Stanley passed away at the age of 76 on 24 May 1984. (Via *Aeroplane*)

between Bristol and SNECMA, because the French manufacturer was building the Bristol Hercules engines under licence in France. Consequently, in 1961, when the two countries decided to build the SST together, this understanding worked in favour of the programme, although it was never plain sailing with any part of the joint venture. Stanley Hooker was given the task of selecting the team to develop the Olympus, which would power the new airliner. Originally, aircraft designer Archibald (later Sir) Russell, had conceived the British SST to carry 130 passengers at Mach 2.2 with power from six Olympus engines. This was not accepted by the Bristol board (Bristol Siddeley from 1960), and Russell was urged to reconsider a smaller aircraft to be powered by four engines. He was unhappy with the decision but came up with a suitable replacement that looked more like the final Concorde design. Hooker and Russell worked closely on the SST programme and made rapid changes as the design progressed and altered, including reducing the maximum speed of the aircraft to Mach 2.0. This was only decided upon after extensive tests by Shell on the fuel and oil systems and how they reacted to the proposed speed.

Taking the Olympus Mk 320 from the TSR.2 as a basis for development, the team started work, in 1964, on what would emerge as the Olympus Mk 593. As noted, the engine was a twin spool engine but by now had seven compressor stages on each spool. Unusually, the first compressor stage was made of titanium, and the last four compressor stages were made of nickel alloy owing to the high pressures and thus high temperatures in supersonic flight. Ordinarily, nickel alloy is only used on the turbine sections of jet engines. Although Hooker was in overall control of Bristol Siddeley Engines, it was Pierre Young who consulted Hooker and who was in charge of the Olympus Mk 593 team. Stanley Hooker later wrote: 'We started by giving the Olympus (593) a zero-stage on the front LP compressor to pump more air with a higher pressure ration, as well as a redesigned turbine with air-cooled rotor blades to allow a higher operating temperature. However, there is a limit to this path and we were running out of steam at around 30,000lbs of thrust. The Concorde, however, was obviously heading for a minimum requirement of 36,000lbs of thrust per engine.'

Bristol Siddeley was responsible for the complicated engine intake arrangement, one that was not without its problems and one that was sorted out by the exceptional team of engineers at Filton. SNECMA held complete responsibility for the back end of the engine nozzles, and the two teams had to work closely in getting this right. Stanley Hooker stated that, while there were problems, he could not recall '…a single technical difference that was not settled by a single short meeting. The French were not keen on reheating in the jet pipe but if Concorde was to take-off fully loaded we had to use afterburning'. Meetings were held in Britain and France, and the airframe design teams were unhappy with the use of reheat in a commercial airliner. There were complications in having a variable propelling nozzle and extra noise. There was also a higher fire risk. All these factors had to be considered and dealt with accordingly by the airframe and engine design teams. Discussions about the engines were held, and SNECMA's lead engineers, Michel Garnier and Jean Devriese, took it upon themselves to sort out the reheat. SNECMA used an Olympus Mk 301 in testing scale models of the nozzle system. Hooker remembered that '…they produced a superb reheat and nozzle system which gave Concorde that smooth transition to supersonic flight'.

The hard-working and long-serving Vulcan B.1 XA903, which was used as an engine test bed for virtually its entire career, which lasted from 1957 to 1979. The bomber flight-tested the Olympus Mk 593 from 1966, and, after 219 flights, the trials were completed in 1971, after 420hrs of testing. (Via Martyn Chorlton)

A 32,825lb (dry), 34,370lb (reheat) Bristol Siddeley/SNECMA Olympus 593-3B being installed into Concorde 001 at Toulouse on 12 July 1968. (Via *Aeroplane*)

Under Rolls-Royce ownership

The Olympus Mk 593B was first run in November 1965. The B was a redesign of the Mk 593D, which was planned for an earlier, smaller Concorde design and which had been tested to supply information for the larger engine. The B was dropped later from the designation. Rolls-Royce acquired Bristol Siddeley Engines in 1966 and continued with the programme; this move brought Hooker back into the fold and also gave him the opportunity to work with some of his former Rolls-Royce colleagues. The merger brought many talented engineers together.

In June 1966, a complete Olympus Mk 593 engine and variable geometry exhaust assembly was first run at Melun-Villaroche in France and at Bristol, flight tests of the Olympus Mk 593 commenced using an RAF Vulcan with the engine attached to its underside. Owing to the Vulcan's aerodynamic limitations, the tests were limited to a speed of Mach 0.98. During these tests, the Olympus achieved 35,190lb of thrust, which exceeded the requirements of the engine. Later in 1966, the Olympus Mk 593 delivered 37,000lb of thrust with the use of the afterburners. In April 1967, the Olympus Mk 593 ran for the first time in a high-altitude chamber at Saclay Ile-de-France, and, in January 1968, the Vulcan flying test bed logged 100 flight hours. That same month, the variable geometry exhaust assembly for the Olympus Mk 593 engine was cleared at Melun-Villaroche for flight in Concorde prototypes.

Brian Trubshaw remembered the problems with the early tests of the Mk 593 engine:

> It had a propensity to break shafts, which was due to the temperature differences between top and bottom during cooling after engine shutdown. On re-start the out of balance shaft could break. The engineers sorted this problem out in later years with an additional bearing but even after we were flying the prototypes, we had to be careful with engine temperatures. We also had a problem with excessive exhaust smoke with the early engines. This was partly cured by changing the cannular combustion chamber to an annular vaporising type and though that cured the smoke the vaporisers used to fall off on a regular basis. This meant the engine had to be changed and this happened quite often during the various proving flights of the prototypes before the aircraft went into service.

There were plans for quieter and more powerful versions of the engine, the Olympus Mk 622, with an extra turbine section and a larger-diameter air compressor that would have eschewed the reheat and added sound-deadening. Rolls-Royce was confident that this would have improved efficiency across

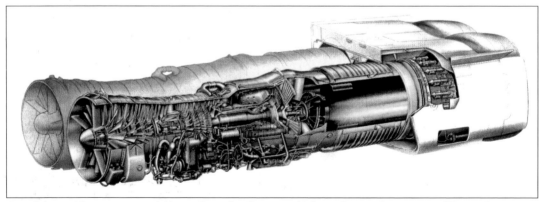

One of the world's most successful jet engines, the Olympus, which was first run in 1950, is well known in Britain as the power behind the Vulcan and the most powerful engine ever to be installed into a civilian airliner. (Martyn Chorlton)

the board, giving Concorde greater range and opening up new routes, particularly across the Pacific, as well as transcontinental routes across America. However, though designs were well advanced, the engine was not proceeded with when it became clear that Concorde was not going to be ordered in quantity by the major world airlines. An interesting aside was made by Sir Stanley Hooker who said: 'When you compare the Olympus Mk 593 with Frank Whittle's flight engine of 1943, it weighs seven times as much and gives 25 times the thrust, up to three times the speed and with much lower specific fuel consumption. We talked with Whittle during the design stages of the Concorde engine; he was most interested in progress and made several useful suggestions.'

Until Concorde's regular commercial flights ceased, the Olympus was unique in aviation as the only afterburning turbojet powering a commercial aircraft. When the Olympus was flown in Concorde at Mach 2.0 it was, at the time, the most efficient jet engine in the world.

Detail of the large under-fuselage pod, which was emblazoned with 'Bristol Siddeley SNECMA Olympus'. The smaller pod between the port No. 1 and No. 2 engines is an Armstrong Siddeley Viper, also under test. (Via Martyn Chorlton)

Chapter 4

Prototypes, Pre-Production and Development

The first prototype – Concorde 001

With the first metal cut in April 1965, the first Concorde reached the final assembly stage at Toulouse in April 1966, underwent resonance testing in August 1967 and, in front of 1,100 guests, was first rolled out of its hangar at Toulouse on 11 December 1967. It was at this event that the late Tony Wedgwood Benn, the British Technology Minister, announced that the British aircraft would be named Concorde (with the 'e' on the end), the 'e' he said would stand for 'excellence, England, Europe and entente'.

Preliminary engine testing was carried out in March 1968, and taxi trials began in August 1968. The first prototype Concorde, fitted out with over ten tons of instrumentation, carried out its maiden flight at 1540hrs on 2 March 1969. This historic event was carried out by Aérospatiale test pilot André

Turcat with Jacques Guignard as co-pilot, Michel Retief as the flight engineer and three flight test observers. The aircraft, registered as F-WTSS but forever known as 001, was flown manually with the undercarriage and nose down during the 42-minute flight, which ended with a perfect landing back at Toulouse at 1608hrs. Concorde 001 then embarked on its long flight test programme, although this was interrupted on 29 May 1969 when the airliner made a low pass over Paris before joining Concorde 002 at the Paris Air Show for their first official appearance together before the public.

001 performed its first tentative supersonic flight on 1 October 1969 during its 45th test flight. At 36,000ft, positioned 75 miles from Toulouse, the airliner maintained Mach 1.05 for nine minutes from 1129hrs; this was the first of 249 flights that would see 001 breach the sound barrier. On 8 November, several pilots from Air France, BOAC, Pan Am and TWA took turns flying 001; the presence of the American crews would have been most encouraging to Aérospatiale/BAC.

On 4 November 1970, the prototype breached Mach 2 for the first time, and all of those who were involved in the project could finally begin to relax as Concorde had reached its required operating speed. By January 1971, flying at supersonic speeds had already become routine with 100 flights between 001 and 002 already having been chalked up. On 13 May, another milestone was reached when 001 carried the first fully automatic landing and, on 25 May, after appearing at the Paris Air Show again, Concorde carried out a 2,500-mile flight to Dakar in 2hrs 7mins.

Concorde 001 carried out a two-week tour of South America in September 1971, which began with the airliner's first transatlantic flight. 001 visited Rio via the Cape Verde islands, Cayenne and

The very first Concorde flight, performed by 001 F-WTSS on 2 March 1969, flown by André Turcat and Jacques Guignard, in company with a Centre d'Essais en Vol Meteor NF.11. (Via François Prins)

São Paolo. At Rio, the aircraft was the centrepiece to the 'France 71' exhibition, carrying out several demonstration flights totalling 29hrs 52mins, of which 13hrs 30mins were performed above Mach 1 and 9hrs 21mins above Mach 2.

On 6 January 1972, 001 flew to Fairford to join 002 (G-BSST) and 01 (G-AXDN), and, by May, all three aircraft had totalled 1,000 trouble-free flying hours. June 1973 saw 001 and 002 carry out high-altitude sampling flights as part of an international research programme to gain more knowledge of the stratosphere. 001 also took scientists from Britain, France and the US aloft to view a solar eclipse, predicted to be the longest for 1,000 years. Flying from Las Palmas in the Canaries to Fort Lamy in Chad, 001 flew at 55,000ft, and this enabled the scientists to view the eclipse for 80 minutes. These scientific-related flights highlighted how potentially useful an aircraft with Concorde's performance could be to the scientific community. By late 1973, the aircraft had already reached the end of its short career. On 19 October, 001 was retired to the Air and Space Museum at Le Bourget, where it remains to this day.

HISTORY – 001
MAIDEN FLIGHT: 2 March 1969 from Toulouse
REGISTRATION HISTORY: First registered as F-WTSS to Aérospatiale on 11 December 1967
TOTAL FLIGHTS: 397
TOTAL SUPERSONIC FLIGHTS: 249
TOTAL FLYING HOURS: 812hrs 19mins
TOTAL SUPERSONIC FLYING HOURS: 254hrs 49mins
FINAL FLIGHT: 19 October 1973 to Le Bourget
CURRENT LOCATION: Musée de l'Air et de l'Espace, Le Bourget, Paris

The second prototype – Concorde 002

Just like 001 at Toulouse, the first metal of the British prototype, presented as 002 and registered G-BSST, was cut in the Brabazon hangar at Filton in April 1965. Final assembly was begun in August 1966, and, on 19 September 1968, the aircraft was rolled out for the first time. On 9 April 1969, with BAC chief test pilot Brian Trubshaw at the controls, John Cochrane as co-pilot, Brian Watts as flight engineer, R. Addley, J. C. Allan and P. A. Holding acting as flight test observers, 002, with an all-up weight of 240,000lb (53,000lb of which was fuel), began rolling down Filton's 9,000ft-long main runway. At 175kts to 180kts, Trubshaw rotated 002 and, with exactly half of the runway used up, was off the ground at 1424hrs, climbing away at 220kts to the west over the Severn estuary before turning on an easterly heading for Fairford at 3,000ft. In company with Canberra B.2 WJ627 borrowed from the Radar Research Establishment (RRE) for Concorde chase duties, 002 levelled out at 9,000ft. Trubshaw then began his brief flight test programme, which was to carry out three airspeed checks with the accompanying Canberra and a few gentle turns to get a feel of how well the aircraft handled; both tasks were carried out satisfactorily. In no time at all, the next stage of this short flight was to set the aircraft up for the approach to Fairford. Auto-throttles were engaged, and 002 was positioned by Brize Norton radar, which controlled the airspace around Fairford. At 2,500ft, 002 levelled out to join Fairford's base leg, which called for small adjustment in the aircraft's course when a light aircraft was spotted close by. Without fuss or drama, 002 was lined up on approach and speed was reduced to 170kts. Both radio altimeters failed during the flight so Trubshaw's very first landing would be totally by eye but with only the smallest bounce on touchdown, the giant brake parachute deployed and, reverse thrust engaged, 002 was put down on Fairford's 10,000ft runway with no difficulty at all, 22 minutes after leaving Filton.

Just like 001 in France, 002 embarked on its flight test programme with key moments being achieved in rapid succession. 002 breached Mach 1 for the first time on 25 March 1970 and Mach 2 on 12 November. The same year, 002 attended the SBAC at Farnborough on 1 September and, on the 13th, landed at Heathrow for the first time giving local residents cause to complain about the noise; one of many issues that would never leave Concorde. On 7 February 1972, 002 flew with a production type undercarriage and, in April, made its debut in Germany at the Hanover Air Show on 22–23 April. Like 001, 002 embarked on its own sales/demonstration tour after leaving Fairford on 2 June for a 45,000-mile-long tour of 12 countries across the Far East and on to Australia, returning to Heathrow on 1 July.

002 was heavily involved in 'hot and high' airfield performance trials during 1973 (beginning with a flight to Jan Smuts Airport, Johannesburg, on 22 January), which were completed on 20 February. Back at Fairford four days later, further temperature and altitude accountability trials were carried out on 9 July, using the Spanish airport at Torrejon, which was 2,000ft a.m.s.l., as its operating base. While 002 continued to carry out trials work, by 1974 and into 1975, the British prototype had been pushed out of the limelight when the development and eventual production aircraft began to take over. With BA already taking delivery of their first aircraft, 002 was retired on 4 March 1976 when, appropriately, Brian Trubshaw flew the aircraft to the Fleet Air Arm Museum at Yeovilton.

Concorde 002 G-BSST is rolled out of the Brabazon hangar at Filton on 19 September 1968. (Via Martyn Chorlton)

HISTORY – 002

MAIDEN FLIGHT: 9 April 1969 from Filton

REGISTRATION HISTORY: First registered as G-BSST on 6 May 1968 to UK Ministry of Technology; reregistered as G-BSST on 19 February 1971 to Ministry of Aviation Supply; reregistered as G-BSST on 26 July 1976 to London Science Museum

TOTAL FLIGHTS: 438

TOTAL SUPERSONIC FLIGHTS: 196

TOTAL FLYING HOURS: 836hrs 9mins

TOTAL SUPERSONIC FLYING HOURS: 173hrs 26mins

FINAL FLIGHT: 4 March 1976 to Yeovilton

CURRENT LOCATION: Fleet Air Arm Museum, RNAS Yeovilton, Somerset

Concorde 002 at Heathrow in 1974, the last time the British prototype would visit the airport. The first time that the supersonic airliner visited the airport, it caused protest from the locals regarding the noise but was destined to be a familiar sight for nearly 30 years. (Via Martyn Chorlton)

Concorde 002 during early flight trials, which continued intensely from the aircraft's maiden flight on 9 April 1969 through to 1974. (Via François Prins)

TECHNICAL DATA – PROTOTYPE 001 & 002

ENGINES: Four 32,825lb (dry), 34,370lb (reheat) Bristol Siddeley/SNECMA Olympus 593-3B turbojets

LENGTH: 184ft 4½in (56.12m)

WINGSPAN: 83ft 10in (25.55m)

HEIGHT: 36ft 6in (11.12m)

FUSELAGE INTERNAL LENGTH*: 129ft (39.32m)

FUSELAGE MAX INTERNAL WIDTH*: 8ft 7½in (2.62m)

FUSELAGE MAX INTERNAL HEIGHT*: 6ft 5in (1.95m)

PASSENGERS: 100 to 138

MAX SPEED: Mach 2.2

INITIAL CLIMB RATE: 5,000ft/min

CEILING: 65,000ft

RANGE: 4,200 miles with max fuel and 3,390 miles with max payload

* The fuselage figures are applicable to all Concordes

The first pre-production aircraft – Concorde 01/101

On the day that 002 (G-BSST) was rolled out of the Brabazon hangar at Filton in September 1968, engineers were only briefly distracted, as they continued to work on the first pre-production Concorde 101 (original known as 01), registered as G-AXDN. The pre-production Concordes were the next stepping stone towards the more familiar production aircraft that graced the world for so many years. Features included a different wing plan form, the ability to carry extra fuel, a higher standard of engine, and later, a modified intake system, a new 'droop-snoot' nose, a transparent visor and a fuselage that was 9ft longer.

While rolled out at Filton on 20 September 1971, 101 carried out its maiden flight from Filton to Fairford, once again in the hands of Trubshaw and Cochrane, on 17 December. 101 went supersonic for the first time on 12 February 1972, but at this stage in the aircraft's career, it was limited to Mach 1.5. The reason for this was that the engine intakes were fixed because of a decision to upgrade the system's control equipment from analogue to a digital. The latter work began on 10 August as part of an overall modification programme that included installation of the latest Olympus 593 Mk 2 production standard engines. The digitally controlled variable geometry intakes were also fitted, and the leading edges of the wing were modified to improve their aerodynamic performance. All of this work was completed by early 1973, and, on 15 March, 101 returned to Fairford to continue the flight test programme.

Early 1974 began with a trip to Tangier on 8 January for intake performance trials, returning to Fairford on 13 January. 101 returned to Tangier on 26 March for further trials after the intake control system was modified. Now completely unrestricted, 101 recorded a speed of Mach 2.23 at 63,700ft during testing. 101 spent most of June 1974 at Toulouse (the home of the French-built Concorde) to test several different types of water deflectors, which were attached to the undercarriage and were all designed to stop water from a wet runway being ingested into the intakes.

After taking part in the 1974 SBAC at Farnborough in September, 101 set for Bangor, Maine, on 7 November, flying directly from Fairford in a record-breaking time of 2hrs 56mins. This was the fastest east-west crossing of the North Atlantic by a commercial airliner by a considerable margin. The main objective of the flight was to test how efficient the aircraft's de-icing system was, and to help achieve this, a small closed-circuit TV system was fitted to the outside of the aircraft, relaying its pictures to a station at the rear of the cabin. A further flight was made from Bangor to Moses, Washington, on the west coast of America in 4hrs 43min, another record-breaking time for an east to west crossing of the US. The return journey, carried out on 11 December, was even quicker, the 2,500-mile flight was covered in just 3hrs 50mins. Two days later, 101 was back at Fairford, covering

The first pre-production Concorde 101, G-AXDN, touching down at Fairford during an early test flight in 1972. The aircraft was delivered to Duxford by Brian Trubshaw and John Cochrane on 20 August 1977. (Via François Prins)

HISTORY – 101

MAIDEN FLIGHT: 17 December 1971 from Filton to Fairford

REGISTRATION HISTORY: First registered as G-AXDN on 16 April 1969 to UK Ministry of Technology; reregistered as G-AXDN on 19 February 1971 to Ministry of Aviation Supply; reregistered as G-AXDN on 20 August 1977 on delivery to the Duxford Aviation Society; de-registered by the CAA on 10 November 1986

TOTAL FLIGHTS: 273

TOTAL SUPERSONIC FLIGHTS: 168

TOTAL FLYING HOURS: 574hrs 49mins

TOTAL BLOCK HOURS*: 632hrs 56min

TOTAL SUPERSONIC FLYING HOURS: 217hrs (over Mach 1) and 170hrs (over Mach 2)

MAX SPEED ATTAINED: Mach 2.23 (1,450mph)

MAX HEIGHT REACHED: 63,700ft

FINAL FLIGHT: 20 August 1977, Filton to Duxford

CURRENT LOCATION: IWM Museum, Duxford, Cambridgeshire

A block hour applies from the moment an aircraft is pushed back from a departure gate to the point it reaches the arrival gate

the North Atlantic in the exact same time that it had achieved on 7 November. Tropical icing trials were carried out at Nairobi from 26 February 1975, and 101 returned to Fairford on 12 March. On 15 May, all test and development flying that had been allocated to 101 had been completed and the aircraft was placed in storage at Fairford.

When the Fairford test centre was closed down, 101 was flown to Filton on 21 January 1977, and once again placed, briefly, into storage. By the summer, there was much talk about the future of 101 and a home was secured at Duxford for the aircraft. In August, the aircraft was prepared for its final flight, which involved borrowing an engine to bring 101 up to an airworthy standard. On 18 August, flight testing was carried out from Filton, and several test landings were made to make sure that the aircraft could be brought safely to a stop in the space of 6,000ft, which was length of Duxford's main runway. On 20 August, 101 took off from Filton for its final flight to Duxford with Brian Trubshaw and John Cochrane at the controls.

The second pre-production aircraft – Concorde 02/102

Structurally complete in February 1972 at Toulouse, the fourth Concorde to be built and second pre-production aircraft was registered as F-WTSA in April 1971. This aircraft represented the shape of the production aircraft with its extended tail cone, increased span and secondary engine nozzles complete with thrust reverser buckets. F-WTSA was also the first Concorde to be fitted with the Olympus 593 Mk 602 engine, which was delivered to Toulouse in April 1972. F-WTSA was rolled out at Toulouse on 28 September 1972 and carried out its maiden flight on 10 January 1973.

On 23 February, the French wasted no time in displaying the potential of a production Concorde when F-WTSA carried a 3,728-mile non-stop return from Toulouse to Iceland in just 3hrs 27mins, with 2hrs 9mins of the journey being performed at Mach 2. The distance covered was the equivalent to a flight from Paris to New York, and it was clear from the outset which of the routes Concorde would be most at home on. On 3 March, F-WTSA made similar 'equivalent' flight when it flew from Toulouse to West Africa in 3hrs 38mins; replicating a journey from Frankfurt to New York.

On 18 September 1973, F-WTSA, displaying British Airways makings on one side of the fuselage and Air France on the other, made history when the airliner flew from Paris to the US, via Las Palmas and Caracas, to arrive for the opening of the Dallas/Fort Worth International Airport on 20 September. Six days later, F-WTSA left for Paris from Washington with 32 passengers on board in a record time of 3hrs 33mins.

The less glamorous but still important task of carrying out 'cold soak' trials was next on the agenda for F-WTSA. This trial was successfully carried out at Fairbanks, Alaska, between 7 and 19 February 1974. The glamour returned on 5 June, when F-WTSA made a 12,000-mile return trip from Paris to Rio de Janeiro in 12hrs 47mins, followed by a tour of the Americas between 20 and 28 October. Setting out via Heathrow and Gander, F-WTSA went on to tour the North and South American Pacific coast taking in Mexico City, via San Francisco, Anchorage, Los Angeles, Lima, Bogotá and Caracas, before heading back through Las Palmas to Paris.

F-WTSA took part in several days' worth of water deflector trials on a flooded runway from 3 March 1975 and, on 30 May, was on static display alongside F-WTSB at the Paris Air Show. It was back in the limelight again on 4 October, when the aircraft was flown from Paris to Montreal, via London and Ottawa, to steal the show for the opening of Mirabel International Airport. F-WTSA flew its 313th and final test flight on 29 January 1976. However, this was not F-WTSA's final flight; on 20 May 1976, Concorde took off from Toulouse at 1519hrs and touched down at Paris Orly Airport at 1626hrs as a static exhibit in place of a full-size wooden replica, which had been burned by vandals. Engines and a large number of valuable components were removed, all test equipment was stripped from the cabin to be replaced by seats to represent an 'in service' aircraft. For many years, F-WTSA stood at Orly alongside the prototype Caravelle 01, but, by 1986, the owners of the airport had lost interest in these

Concorde 002 F-WTSA arriving at Prestwick from Ottawa in October 1975. (Mark Piacentini)

F-WTSA, with the original Air France scheme on the port side and British Airways markings on the starboard, is taxiing at Prestwick in February 1974, bound for Fairbanks, Alaska, for 'cold soak' trials. (Mark Piacentini)

HISTORY – 102
MAIDEN FLIGHT: 10 January 1973 from Toulouse
REGISTRATION HISTORY: First registered as F-WTSA to Aerospatoale on 21 April 1971
TOTAL FLIGHTS: 314
TOTAL SUPERSONIC FLIGHTS: 189
TOTAL BLOCK HOURS: 656hrs 37mins
TOTAL SUPERSONIC FLYING HOURS: 280hrs 49mins
FINAL TEST FLIGHT: 29 January 1976
FINAL FLIGHT: 20 May 1976 to Orly
CURRENT LOCATION: Musée Delta, Orly Airport, Paris

two important aircraft, and they were condemned to scrap. The Caravelle could not be saved, but, thanks to the efforts of the Athis Aviation Association, F-WTAS was saved and today can be seen at the Musée Delta, Athis-Mons, just south of Orly airport, where it has resided since 12 April 1988.

The first development aircraft – Concorde 201

The first of two development aircraft was 201 F-WTSB, which made its maiden flight on 6 December 1973. Such was the confidence with Concorde by this stage that the first flight lasted for 2hrs 40mins and a speed of Mach 1.57 was reached. A great deal of the pre-service flying was carried out by the development aircraft and several subtle changes were incorporated, which were mainly structural.

Flight testing included intake control work, which was carried out from Casablanca, Morocco, in October 1974, and a spell of endurance trials began from 9 June 1975. The latter included flights to Bodø, Dakar, Shannon and Tangier and subsonic flights in France to Charles de Gaulle, Lille, Lyon, Marseilles and Nice. F-WTSB contributed to Concorde's historical landmarks when it became the first example to land in New York on 19 October 1977 for a set of proving flights.

F-WTSB was flown regularly until 1982, having quickly accumulated over 900hrs of block time. Stored in an airworthy condition at Chateauroux, the aircraft made its final flight on 19 April 1985, when it was ferried back to its original home at Toulouse.

HISTORY – 201
MAIDEN FLIGHT: 6 December 1973 from Toulouse
REGISTRATION HISTORY: First registered as F-WTSB to Aérospatiale
TOTAL FLIGHTS: 423
TOTAL SUPERSONIC FLIGHTS: 247
TOTAL BLOCK HOURS: 909hrs 52mins
TOTAL SUPERSONIC FLYING HOURS: 339hrs 25mins
FINAL FLIGHT: 19 April 1985, Chateauroux to Toulouse
CURRENT LOCATION: Musée Aeroscopia, Toulouse

The first development aircraft, Concorde 201 F-WTSB, looking very handsome in the Air France scheme at Toulouse in 1974. After spending many years outside at Toulouse since its final flight in 1985, F-WTSB is now at Musée Aeroscopia, France. (Martyn Chorlton)

The second development aircraft – Concorde 202

Registered as G-BBDG on 7 August 1973, Concorde 202, the second development aircraft and the final aircraft of the entire development fleet, lifted off from Filton's runway for the first time on 13 February 1974, travelling for 1hr 45mins and landing at Fairford. Just like F-WTSB before it, supersonic speeds were confidently achieved from the outset.

On 7 August, Brian Trubshaw and crew departed Heathrow Airport on a high-speed run to Tehran, where several passengers disembarked. G-BBDG was then flown to Bahrain where hot weather trials and general ground testing were carried out. With the trials successfully completed, G-BBDG embarked on a demonstration tour across the Middle East from 27 August, which stopped in Abu Dhabi, Dubai, Kuwait, Muscat and Qatar. On 3 September, G-BBDG departed Bahrain bound for Singapore, where runway response trials were carried out.

In company with F-WTSB, G-BBDG arrived at Casablanca on 28 October, where take-off noise levels were measured and supersonic cruise checks in cold air were made as part of the certification

HISTORY – 202
MAIDEN FLIGHT: 13 February 1974 from Filton to Fairford
REGISTRATION HISTORY: First registered as G-BBDG on 7 August 1973 to BAC; de-registered
TOTAL FLIGHTS: 633
TOTAL SUPERSONIC FLIGHTS: 374
TOTAL FLYING HOURS: 1282hrs 09mins
TOTAL BLOCK HOURS: 1435hrs 3min
TOTAL SUPERSONIC FLYING HOURS: 514hrs 9mins
FINAL FLIGHT: 24 December 1981, Filton to Filton
CURRENT LOCATION: Brooklands Museum, Weybridge, Surrey, arrived May and June 2004

The first Concorde to carry over 100 passengers at twice the speed of sound was the second development aircraft, Concorde 202 G-BBDG, which remained a trials aircraft from its maiden flight in 1974 to its last in 1981. (Martyn Chorlton)

testing. Acknowledged as the fastest of the development aircraft, G-BBDG was the first Concorde to carry 100 passengers at the twice the speed of sound.

Even once the main production versions were in service, G-BBDG kept flying to trial and test various performance enhancements, including a redesigned air intake that needed certification. Coupled with more powerful engines, the air intake modification achieved an increase in payload of up to 2,000lb. G-BBDG was also used to trial the 2in extension of the control surface trailing edge.

G-BBDG made its final landing at Filton on 24 December 1981, where it remained in airworthy condition until 1983, in readiness for additional development work or general test flying. G-BBDG was purchased by BA in 1984 in order to provide spares for the rest of its fleet. In 1988, BA constructed a hangar at Filton to protect G-BBDG, as more internal components were returned to the air. When G-BOAF's nose was damaged in 1995, G-BBDG's droop nose was used as a replacement, and, in 2002, the airframe was used to test strengthened cockpit doors, which had to be introduced after the terrorist attacks on 11 September 2001. Following the retirement of the BA fleet, G-BBDF was offered to Brooklands Museum in October 2003. The aircraft was dismantled and, during May and June 2004, was delivered by road in large sections. The aircraft has been on display since 2006 and now sports the restored nose of G-BOAF, which was also donated to the museum in 2005.

PRE-PRODUCTION, TECH INFO
ENGINES: Four 32,520lb (dry), 35,080lb (reheat) Bristol Siddeley/SNECMA Olympus 593-4 turbojets
LENGTH: 194ft (59.13m)
WINGSPAN: 83ft 10in (25.55m)
HEIGHT: 38ft (11.58m)
PASSENGERS: 100 to 148
MAX SPEED: Mach 2.2
INITIAL CLIMB RATE: 5,000ft/min
CEILING: 60,000ft
RANGE: 3,550 miles with max fuel and 3,390 miles with max payload

The second pre-production Concorde, F-WTSA, carries out its maiden flight in the hands of André Turcat from Toulouse on 10 January 1973. (Via *Aeroplane*)

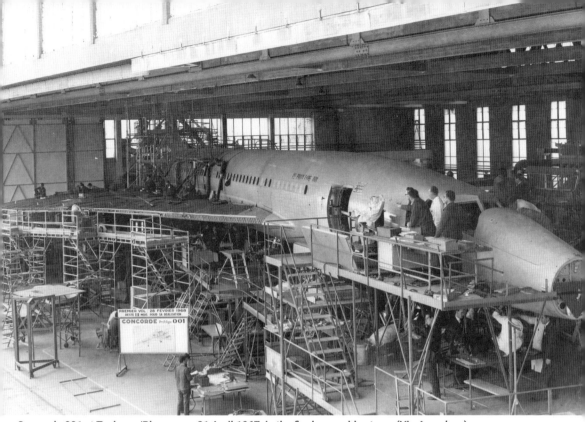

Concorde 001 at Toulouse/Blagnac on 21 April 1967, in the final assembly stage. (Via *Aeroplane*)

As Concorde 002 reaches the final stages of its construction, the first pre-production Concorde 01 takes shape in the foreground on 3 May 1968. All of the French-built components for 01 were delivered from factories at Bouguenais, Marignane, Toulouse and St Nazaire. (BAC via Martyn Chorlton)

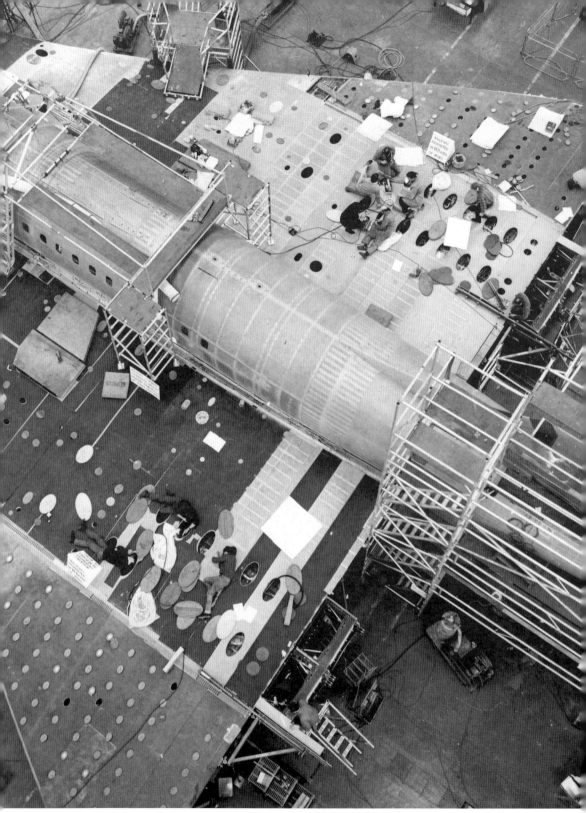

An excellent vertical view of Concorde 002 at Filton, seemingly strewn with engineers in various positions, highlighting just how difficult this complex machine was to build. (Associated Press Photo via Martyn Chorlton)

Concorde 002 pictured at Filton in August 1968 after it was lowered from the jacks that had supported the airliner during the installation of systems and various equipment. The next stage would be the final phase of fuel transference tests prior to the first engine runs. (BAC via Martyn Chorlton)

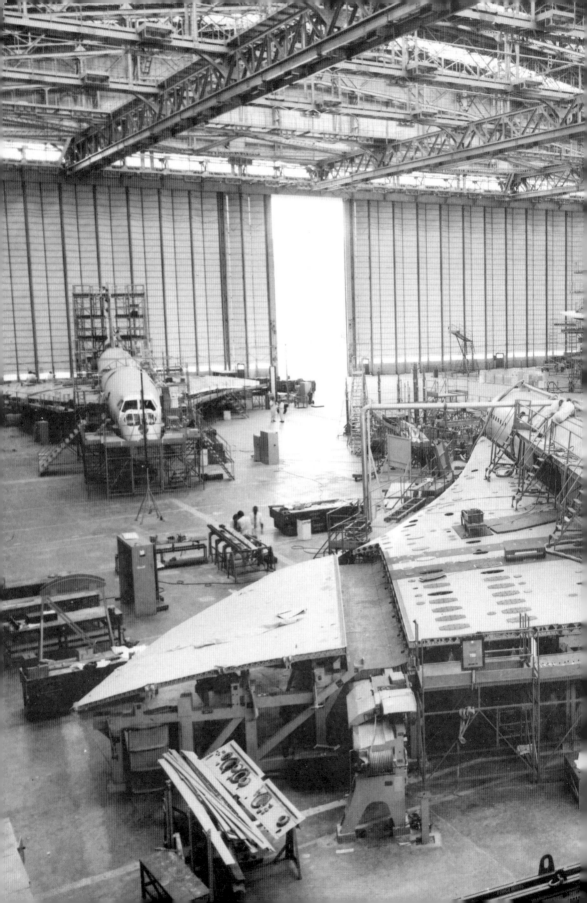

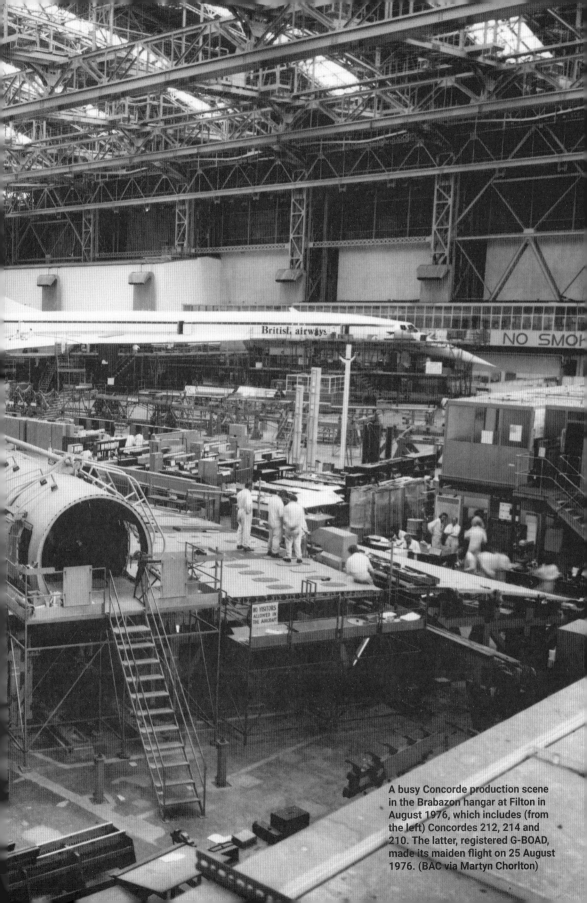

A busy Concorde production scene in the Brabazon hangar at Filton in August 1976, which includes (from the left) Concordes 212, 214 and 210. The latter, registered G-BOAD, made its maiden flight on 25 August 1976. (BAC via Martyn Chorlton)

Concorde 001 F-WTSS is in the
background at Toulouse, looking over
the second pre-production Concorde
02/101, registered F-WTSA, in April 1971.
(Via François Prins)

Chapter 5
Air France

Pre-history

Formed on 7 October 1933 by merging five major French airlines that had already established
an extensive network of routes through France and the colonies in North Africa, Air France was
nationalised in June 1945. Post-war, as with most airlines, the main type operated was the Douglas
DC-3/C-47, but the purchase of several long-range DC-4s opened up the opportunity for the first
flights from Paris to New York, which, after two refuelling stops, could be achieved in a little under
20hrs. Air France grew quickly and, by 1948, had 130 aircraft to its name, and with the arrival of
the Lockheed Constellation the previous year, the airline continued to expand its global network.
From 1952, Air France bought British for the first time in the shape of the de Havilland Comet I,
which momentarily launched the airline into the jet age, only to be grounded because of structural
failures. The Vickers Viscount followed but, from 1960, the airline's domestic operations were diluted
and transferred to Air Inter on the condition that Air France was given a large stake in the airline.

**Although F-WTSB never actually served with Air
France, it wore the crisp company livery throughout
its career. (Air France via Martyn Chorlton)**

The airline settled into jet operations with the arrival of the Boeing 707 and the Sud Caravelle, later complemented by the Boeing 727 and the 747 (Air France went on to have one of the largest 747 fleets). Air France also took delivery of the first Airbus A300 in 1974, built by Airbus Industrie in another example of international co-operation, which had grown into the only serious challenger to the all-conquering Boeings.

A foot hold in the states

Many years before the first metal was cut, Air France, along with BA and Pan American, placed a pre-order for six Concordes on 3 June 1963. This order was increased to eight aircraft in 1965, and then reduced to four aircraft on 24 July 1972, which stood until the first Concorde was delivered.

The first aircraft to be delivered to Air France's main base at Charles de Gaulle airport was F-BVFA on 19 December 1975. It was the intention to despatch F-BVFA on the inaugural route from Paris to New York, but, because of a ban placed upon Concorde by the US government, the airline decided to fly from Charles de Gaulle to Rio de Janeiro instead, with a fuel stop at Dakar, Senegal. The flight took place on 26 January 1976, the same day BA inaugurated its Concorde services from London to Bahrain. From 10 April, by which time F-BTSC (leased) and F-BVFB had been delivered, services were begun to Caracas, Venezuela, using the Azores as a fuel stop. Air France continued a scheduled service to Caracas and Rio until April 1982.

Power-dressing business-types being catered for in this publicity shot of a Concorde cabin, taken in the 1980s. (Air France)

The majority of promotional photographs of a Concorde 'at work' would show at least one of the cabins serving high-class food or expensive alcohol. (Air France)

In the meantime, the battle continued in the US to stop Concorde from operating there, with at least 40 objections (including the aircraft's effect on the ozone layer) being placed and quoted from the Federal Air Regulations. The final decision was in the hands of US Secretary of Transportation William T. Coleman, Jr., who only focused on two of the objections that raised the issue of noise. On 4 February 1976, both Air France and BA enjoyed a partial victory when Coleman authorised the two airlines to conduct a 16-month demonstration of Concorde, with four flights per day to John F. Kennedy International Airport, New York, and two flights to Dulles International Airport, Washington, DC, the latter beginning on 24 May 1976. However, the city of New York's Port Authority created a local ban of Concorde because of the potential for excessive noise. This final barrier was finally overturned on 17 October, and the first flight by Concorde from Paris to New York took place on 22 November, taking a mere 3hrs 23minutes. As mentioned earlier, the main thrust of the anti-Concorde campaign was noise but following a survey it was found, embarrassingly for the protestors, that the president's own Air Force One (a Boeing VC-137) was louder during take-off and landing and at subsonic speed!

Boom and bust

Two more Concordes, F-BVFC and F-NVFD, were delivered to Air France on 3 August 1976 and 26 March 1977 respectively followed by F-BTSD which was leased from Aérospatiale from 18 September 1977. With more aircraft available, the airline expanded its Concorde operations from September 1978. The new destination was Mexico, which was experiencing an oil boom at the time. Departing from Mexico City's Benito Juárez International Airport, Concorde continued north east to either Washington or New York and then on to Paris. Speed restrictions in place over the US meant that, after taking off Benito Juárez and accelerating over the Gulf of Mexico, the airliner had to decelerate to below Mach 1 once over Florida so as not cause a sonic boom over American soil. Once off the eastern coast of the USA,

An Air France stewardess begins to serve the first round of goodies while the aircraft smoothly accelerates through Mach 1.27 (967mph). (Air France)

the airliner would accelerate back up to Mach 2 before decelerating again to land at Washington or New York. The end of the oil boom combined with a worldwide economic crisis saw the Mexican route come to a conclusion in November 1982, having made little or no profit whatsoever. Concorde would return to Mexico but only for more profitable charter flights to Mexico City and Acapulco, where every seat was taken.

Four Air France and five BA Concordes were leased by Braniff International Airways in 1978. The aircraft were flown below Mach 1 by Braniff crews between Dallas/Fort Worth and Dulles and then supersonically across the Atlantic to London or Paris by the Air France and BA crews. Each Concorde gained its own US registration, while the European registration was covered over when the airliner was flown with Braniff crews. None were painted in full Braniff colours, despite the amount of marketing material showing the aircraft in the company's orange livery. The Braniff routes were never profitable, and the only US operator of Concorde had to give up on the idea in May 1980. A few months later, Air France took delivery of its seventh and final Concorde, F-BVFF, on 23 October.

Reduced services more charters

Air France reduced its scheduled services during the 1980s but increased the more profitable charter flights and, like BA, was never shy of any marketing opportunity that would keep the aircraft in the public eye. Those who could afford to fly on Concorde on an Air France scheduled flight would not enjoy the same features of a long-haul flight, such as in-flight entertainment and reclining seats. However, the three hours that the rich and famous would spend in an Air France Concorde would still be a luxurious affair from the food and drink point of view alone. A typical Paris to New York menu could include lobster, tenderloin steak, goose foie gras, monkfish and all varieties of expensive alcohol, including Dom Perignon champagne.

F-BTSD is pictured here at Paris Charles de Gaulle Airport after it was unveiled at Gatwick in April 1996. (Manuel Negrerie)

Air France only refitted its Concordes' cabins on one occasion in the 1990s, and, as the aircraft grew older, they felt dated compared to the BA machines, which were refitted more regularly to keep them fresh and modern.

Regular charters became the bread-and-butter work for the Air France Concordes from the early 1990s. US-based Spirit Tours and UK-based Goodwood Travel were two of several travel firms that helped to fill seats; the latter chartering one aircraft for a record circumnavigation in October 1992. Interest was never higher than during the mid-1990s, and it was in October 1994 that Richard Branson approached Air France with a view to lease several Concordes and crews for Virgin Atlantic. Another world record circumnavigation was made by an Air France Concorde on 15 August 1996, and the aircraft was in the headlines again on 2 April 1996, when F-BTSD was unveiled at Gatwick Airport painted in a stunning Pepsi-Cola livery to help promote the soft drink.

AIR FRANCE CHARTER FLIGHT LOCATIONS – 1976–98

Africa – Agadir (Morocco), Antananarivo (Madagascar), Bamako (Mali), Bujumbura (Burundi), Conakry (Guinea), Djerba (off Tunisia), Douala (Cameroon), Djibouti, Kigali (Rwanda), Kinshasa (Democratic Republic of the Congo), Lagos (Nigeria), Lanzarote (Canary Islands), Lomé (Togo), Libreville (Gabon), Lusaka (Zambia), Marrakesh (Morocco), Mauritius, Moroni (Comoros), Ouagadougou (Burkina Faso), Réunion, Robertsville (Liberia), Seychelles, Tangier (Morocco), Tozeur (Tunisia), Tunis (Tunisia) and Yamoussoukro (Côte d'Ivoire)

The Americas – Andrews Air Force Base (US), Anchorage (US), Barreirinhas (Brazil), Brasília (Brazil), Bogotá (Colombia), Buenos Aires (Argentina), Cayenne (French Guiana), Chicago (US), Fort-de-France (Martinique), Hampton (US), Havana (Cuba), Iguassu (Brazil/Argentina), Moncton (Canada), Montevideo (Uruguay), Pointe-à-Pitre (Guadeloupe), Port-au-Prince (Haiti), Quebec (Canada), Recife (Brazil) and Regina (Canada)

Oceania – Darwin (Australia), Easter Island, Hao Island (French Polynesia), Mururoa (French Polynesia), Nouméa (New Caledonia), Papeete (French Polynesia)

Europe – Aarhus (Denmark), Aalborg (Denmark), Albacete (Spain), Badajoz (Spain), Bastia (France), Beauvais (France), Biarritz (France), Brest (France), Cambrai (France), Charleroi (Belgium), Clermont-Ferrand (France), Dijon (France), East Midlands (UK), Épinal (France), Frankfurt (Germany), Grenoble (France), Gothenburg (Sweden), Hamburg (Germany), Ibiza, Ivalo (Finland), Klagenfurt (Austria), Lajes (Portugal), Las Palmas (Spain), Liège (Belgium), Lille (France), Lyon (France), Malta, Marseille (France), Metz (France), Montpellier (France), Mulhouse (France), Nantes (France), Nuremberg (Germany), Ostend (Belgium), Reims (France), Santiago de Compestela (Spain), Tarbes (France), Turku (Finland), Valladolid (Spain) and Vichy (France)

Asia – Abu Dhabi (United Arab Emirates), Ankara (Turkey), Baikonur (Kazakhstan), Bangui (The Philippines), Beirut (Lebanon), Chiang Mai (Thailand), Denpasar (Indonesia), Dhaka (Bangladesh), Dubai (United Arab Emirates), Haifa (Israel), Islamabad (Pakistan), Jakarta (Indonesia), Kathmandu (Nepal), Kish (Iran), Muscat (Oman), Nagasaki (Japan), Novosibirsk (Russia), Osaka (Japan), Sanaa (Yemen), Tehran (Iran), Tianjin (China) and Tokyo (Japan).

Concorde F-BVFA, which carried out its last passenger-carrying flight for Air France on 30 May 2003 from John F. Kennedy (JFK) International Airport, New York, to Charles de Gaulle, Paris. On 12 June, F-BVFA flew back across the Atlantic, destined never to return to France. (Via Martyn Chorlton)

THE AIR FRANCE FLEET – 1976–2003	
F-BTSC	Leased to Air France 6 January 1976; crashed 25 July 2000; 11,989hrs
F-BVFA	Delivered to Air France 19 December 1975; retired 12 June 2003; 17,824hrs
F-BVFB	Delivered to Air France 6 March 1976; retired 24 June 2003; 14,771hrs
F-BVFC	Delivered to Air France 3 August 1976; retired 27 June 2003; 14,332hrs
F-BVFD	Delivered to Air France 26 March 1977; retired 27 May 1982; 5,814hrs
F-BTSD	Leased to Air France 18 September 1978; retired 14 June 2003; 12,974hrs
F-BVFF	Delivered to Air France 23 October 1980; retired 11 June 2000; 12,421hrs

The beginning of the end

The tragic loss of F-BTSC on 25 July 2000 was a colossal body blow, not only to the families of those killed but also to the future of the aircraft itself. All Concordes were grounded following the accident and one, F-BVFC, was about to depart New York but was destined to remain grounded until it returned to France on 21 September. An Anglo-French group set to work, trying to understand what

F-BVFA at Charles de Gaulle, having just arrived from JFK airport in August 1998. (Manuel Negrerie)

went wrong on 25 July 2000, and F-BVFB was used to fly a number of test flights from Istres and, later, Charles de Gaulle. Following a number of expensive modifications, Concorde's manufacturers (now Airbus and BAE Systems) applied for re-certification of the aircraft on 16 August 2001, and, on 24 August, Air France's first modified aircraft, F-BVFB, flew at Mach 1 during a verification flight. Three days later, it carried out a 3½hr flight at its normal cruising speed of Mach 2. On 29 October, F-BVFB carried out an operational assessment to New York and back, and resumed full services on 7 November. This was carried out by F-BTSD (AF002), which departed Paris Charles de Gaulle at 1030hrs local and arrived at New York at 0820hrs (EST).

Air France did not come out to well from the subsequent accident investigation report of the loss of F-BTSC, and many maintenance and operating procedures were modified and updated, which all added to the huge cost of running the Concorde fleet. The media on both sides of the Channel were continually looking for the negative view of Concorde following the accident, and while the crews, engineers, general public and enthusiasts alike had no doubts about the safety of the aircraft, the media's often deluded viewpoint would be heard first and the loudest. With this in mind, the 25th anniversary of Concorde services to New York on 22 November 2002 was a rather subdued affair compared to the open celebration that it should have been. The bad publicity seemed impossible to shake off for Air France, and certainly not helped by F-BTSD having to divert to Halifax, Nova Scotia, following a fuel leak on 18 February 2003. One week later, F-BVFA suffered a rudder delamination, a problem experienced by BA Concordes many years earlier, which had not hit the headlines in the same way.

On 10 April 2003, both Air France and BA announced that Concorde would be carrying out its final scheduled passenger flights in October. Air France later brought this forward to 31 May, and both airlines blamed the post-9/11 slump in air travel, rising costs and the negative effort the loss of F-BTSC had on both airlines. The final Air France passenger flights were duly carried out on 31 May, when F-BTSD (AF001) flew to New York and back and F-BVFB flew a charter over the Bay of Biscay. During June, Air France honoured earlier agreements to preserve a number of aircraft and, on 12 June, F-BVFA flew to Dulles (for the Smithsonian), F-BTSD made the short hop to Le Bourget (Air and Space Museum) on 14 June, and F-BVFB was delivered to Karlsruhe/Baden-Baden (for Sinsheim) on 24 June. The final Air France Concorde flight was made by F-BVFC to Toulouse on 27 June, making a total of 90,125 flying hours.

The US's sole Concorde operator – Braniff International Airways

Braniff was one of many airlines that originally placed an order (for three aircraft) back in 1965 but was forced to reconsider and cancel them in February 1973. Its interest in the aircraft never waned and, in 1978, the Braniff chairman, Harding L. Lawrence, negotiated a deal with the FAA that would see Concorde operate over the US.

To allow the aircraft to be operated in the US, a temporary change of ownership would have to occur every time the aircraft flew a route, as the FAA would not issue a non-US aircraft with a US Certificate of Airworthiness (CoA). Another requirement was that only US-approved documentation was to be carried on each flight, which meant that both the Air France and BA paperwork was relegated to the forward toilet! On top of that, the aircraft's registration had to conform to the standard FAA 'N' number; for example, F-BVFB was reregistered by Air France to N94FB.

Braniff flight crews (three pilots [captains], five co-pilots [first officers] and four flight engineers) were trained in Britain and France and, once in service, the cabin crew were also supplied by Braniff. The crews were trained to fly the aircraft at subsonic speeds, which would be the norm over the US, but part of the training gave the experience of also operating at Mach 2. None of the aircraft were ever painted in Braniff colours, although, if the exercise had been a success, there was every chance that one side of the aircraft would have been painted in the company's orange livery.

Another issue that only affected the BA Concordes was the airline's insurers, who insisted that a captain and a flight engineer remained on the flight deck as observers whilst the aircraft was in the hands of a Braniff crew. Another BA anomaly was that all of its Concorde captains had to retire at 55, while their American counterparts could fly until they hit 60. Therefore, on occasions, a Braniff pilot would be flying the aircraft in the US but would not be allowed to fly over Britain.

The air brushed artwork applied to this 'Braniff' Concorde is pretty convincing, but, in reality, the airline's livery was never applied. Nothing more than a loss-leader for Braniff, the full potential of the aircraft was never realised in the US. (British Aerospace)

The Braniff-crewed service began on 12 January 1979, operating between Dallas/Fort Worth and Dulles, where the Air France or BA crew would take over and return across the Atlantic with the original registration on display. Airspeed over US soil was supposed to be flown at Mach 0.95, but it was not difficult to slip through the speed barrier whilst on a remote section of the flight.

A single fare to fly on a Braniff Concorde was US$154 from February to May 1979 and $194 during September and October. This rose to $227 in 1980, which still only represented approximately 10 per cent more than the average cost for a first-class ticket on a traditional airliner. Despite the tempting price, the Braniff service never made money, and passengers could not be lured from the Boeing 727s that flew the same route without a seat to spare. In comparison, Concorde quite often flew the same route with as few as 15 passengers on board, but the aircraft was worth its weight in gold from a publicity point of view – however, this did not stop the service from coming to an end in May 1980.

There was no shortage of promotional material or merchandise once Braniff got into its stride, but, unfortunately, it was all to no avail and the traditional US passenger would not leave the security of their Boeings! (Martyn Chorlton)

Whether in the air or on the ground, Concorde is a beautiful thing from just about any angle. These three stewardesses are modelling Air France's latest uniforms. (Air France)

Chapter 6

'Speedbird Concorde'

Launching a special service

When the concept of an SST was first presented, BOAC was very interested and, along with Air France and Pan American Airways, placed a 'non-binding' order for six aircraft on 3 June 1963. This was increased to eight aircraft in 1964 and decreased to five on 25 May 1972, by which time, BOAC had been ordered by the government to merge with British European Airways (BEA) to become British Airways on 31 March 1974.

The new airline was as fresh as the new supersonic airliner it was about to receive, and hopes were high for commercial success. The first aircraft, G-BOAA, was presented to BA in an official ceremony on 15 January 1976 at the North Bay, Technical Block B of the airline's engineering base at Heathrow. Only six days later, the aircraft began its first BA commercial flight in the hands of Capt Norman Todd, Capt Brian Calvert and senior flight engineer John Lidiard. The aircraft's destination was Bahrain; while a glamorous location, this was not where BA intended the aircraft to serve. The flight to Bahrain (BA300) had amongst its passengers, HRH Duke of Kent, UK Secretary of State for Trade Peter Shore, Sir George Edwards, Gp Capt Leonard Cheshire and test pilot Brian Trubshaw.

Political objections and local protests regarding sonic booms and the general noise that the airliner created were eventually overcome across the pond, and the first service to the US began on 24 May 1976. This was to Dulles, but it was JFK where BA wanted to be, and this nut was not cracked until 22 November 1977.

A British Airways (BA) Concorde in front of the control tower at Kuwait International Airport during the late 1970s. The Middle East was the carrier's first destination until the red tape was sliced, and Concorde began to fly the routes it was designed for across the Atlantic. (*Aeroplane*)

The hard-working G-BOAC had over 140 flights under its belt as a result of route-proving trials before it was delivered to BA on 13 February 1976. (Via François Prins)

'Speedbird' in profit

While Air France did not give its Concorde fleet a unique call sign, BA maintained a long tradition by using 'Speedbird Concorde', which immediately alerted an air traffic controller to the fact that this airliner was a little different. Throughout Concorde's career with BA, the company livery had been maintained and updated over the years but only once was another airline's colours applied and to just one aircraft, G-BOAD. This was in 1977 when the aircraft was briefly, jointly operated by Singapore Airlines and again in 1979, but as with the US earlier, countries were not happy about the aircraft flying at supersonic speeds over their territory and the idea was abandoned in 1980.

By the early 1980s, the number of unprofitable routes was mounting, and the fact that the fleet was still owned by the government, which was trying to recover its initial investment, did not help the situation. In 1981, Sir John King, the managing director of BA, made the wise decision to purchase the Concorde fleet outright from the government at a cost of £16.5m, which, in many people's eyes at the time, undoubtedly secured the future of supersonic travel. The deal was not completed until 1984, but in the meantime, 1982 saw a continuation of losses that suddenly bottomed out, and, in 1983, BA had its first profitable year for Concorde; £14m was made and this increased to £54m in 1987. The turnaround was partly due to an increase in fares and more available routes, including Miami via Washington DC, Barbados, and an extra flight on top of the daily service already arriving in New York. Profitability took a turn for the worse in the early 1990s but was back up to the £60m mark just before the Paris accident. Post-accident figures still showed that Concorde was financially viable with £50m in profit being achieved in the airliner's last year (to October) of operations.

Concordes began services to the US in May 1976, but the main goal of being able to operate from JFK airport was not achieved until November 1977. (Via *Aeroplane*)

Glamorous numbers

Concorde naturally attracted the rich and famous, who were not only drawn to the glamour of the aircraft but to its ability to get them to their destination twice, if not three times, as fast as a conventional airliner. Prime ministers were not shy of making the most of Concorde, James Callaghan being the first in 1976 when he flew to Puerto Rico for the G7 conference. The aircraft was flown by Capt Peter Duffey, who clearly remembers the media sensation that the aircraft caused at San Juan on arrival. The French president Giscard d'Estaing did not receive the same welcome as he trailed in, several hours behind, in a Boeing 707.

Her Majesty The Queen and Prince Philip flew on Concorde together (Philip had already flown on 001 in January 1972) for the first time on 2 November 1982, and again in February 1984 for a three week tour of the Middle East, which began in Kuwait. Concorde soon became the airliner of choice for the Queen and for the Queen Mother, who celebrated her 85th birthday (6 August 1985) during a flight and is believed to have taken the controls at least once during a test flight. The Queen and Prince Philip also used Concorde for a visit to Barbados in March 1987 and again on a tour of the US, which began in May 1991.

The year 1985 saw Phil Collins exploit the performance of Concorde so that he could take part in the Live Aid concert in Britain and the US equivalent in the same day! Margaret Thatcher flew Concorde to Expo '86 in Vancouver and, on 5 October 1987, BA's one millionth scheduled transatlantic passenger was named as Patrick Mannix of Reuters. Amongst the many celebrations of Concorde's tenth anniversary in BA service, Richard Noble (the land speed record holder at the time) made three Atlantic crossings in a single day on 22 November 1987. One of the many events for Children in Need on 3 December 1993 saw the Bee Gees perform the 'fastest show on earth' over the Bay of Biscay in an effort to raise money for the charity.

BRITISH AIRWAYS CHARTER FLIGHT LOCATIONS – 1976–98

Africa – Abidjan (Côte d'Ivoire), Aswan (Egypt), Cairo (Egypt), Capetown (South Africa), Casablanca (Morocco), Dakar (Senegal), Harare (Zimbabwe), Johannesburg (South Africa), Kilimanjaro (Tanzania), Luxor (Egypt), Marrakesh (Morocco), Mombasa (Kenya), Nairobi (Kenya), Robertsville (Liberia) and Tenerife (Canary Islands)

The Americas – Abbotsford (Canada), Acapulco (Mexico), Albany (US), Antigua and Barbuda, Aruba, Asheville (US), Atlanta (US), Atlantic City (US), Austin (US), Baltimore (US), Bangor (US), Barbados, Battle Creek (US), Bermuda, Boston (US), Buffalo (US), Calgary (Canada), Caracas (Venezuela), Charleston (US), Cincinnati (US), Cleveland (US), Colorado Springs (US), Columbus (US), Dayton (US), Denver (US), Detroit (US), Edmonton (Canada), Fort Lauderdale (US), Fort Myers (US), Goose Bay (Canada), Grand Cayman, Harrisburg (US), Hartford–Springfield (US), Honolulu (US), Houston (US), Indianapolis (US), Jackson (US), Jacksonville (US), Kailua-Kona (US), Kansas City (US), Kingston (Jamaica), Las Vegas (US), Lexington (US), Lima (Peru), Little Rock (US), Lubbock (US), Mexico City (Mexico), Miami (US), Midland-Odessa (US), Montego Bay (Jamaica), Montreal (Canada), Nashville (US), Nassau (the Bahamas), New Orleans (US), Newport (US), New York (US), Oakland (US), Oklahoma City (US), Omaha (US), Ontario (US), Orlando (US), Oshkosh (US), Ottawa (Canada), Philadelphia (US), Phoenix (US), Pittsburgh (US), Portland (US), Port of Spain (Trinidad and Tobago), Providence (US), Puerto Rico and Raleigh (US)

Oceania – Auckland (New Zealand), Brisbane (Australia), Christchurch (New Zealand), Fiji, Guam, Learmonth (Australia), Perth (Australia) and Sydney (Australia)

Europe – Aberdeen (Scotland), Amsterdam (The Netherlands), Ancona (Italy), Athens (Greece), Barcelona (Spain), Basel (Switzerland), Belfast (Northern Ireland), Bergen (Norway), Berlin (Germany), Billund (Denmark), Birmingham (England), Bologna (Italy), Bordeaux (France), Boscombe Down (England), Bournemouth (England), Bratislava (Slovakia), Brize Norton (England), Brussels (Belgium), Budapest (Hungary), Cardiff (Wales), Chateauroux (France), Cologne (Germany), Coltishall (England), Copenhagen (Denmark), Derby (England), Dublin (Ireland), East Midlands (England), Edinburgh (Scotland), Exeter (England), Fairford (England), Farnborough (England), Faro (Portugal), Filton (England), Finningley (England), Gatwick (England), Geneva (Switzerland), Glasgow (Scotland), Graz (Austria), Hanover (Germany), Hatfield (England), Helsinki (Finland), Humberside (England), Istanbul (Turkey), Kangerlussuaq (Greenland), Keflavik (Iceland), Kinloss (Scotland), Larnaca (Cyprus), Leeds (England), Leipzig (Germany), Leuchars (Scotland), Linz (Austria), Lisbon (Portugal), Liverpool (England), Llanbedr (Wales), Luton (England), Luxembourg, Machrihanish (Scotland), Madrid (Spain), Málaga (Spain), Manchester (England), Manston (England), Milan (Italy), Mildenhall (England), Moscow (Russia), Munich (Germany), Münster (Germany), Newcastle (England), Nice (France), Oslo (Norway), Paris (France), Pescara (Italy), Pisa (Italy), Poitiers (France), Porto (Portugal), Prague (Czech Republic), Prestwick (Scotland), Rome (Italy), Rovaniemi (Finland), St Mawgan (England), St Petersburg (Russia), Salzburg (Austria), Seville (Spain), Stavanger (Norway), Stockholm (Sweden), Strasbourg (France), Teesside (England) Toulouse (France), Tours (France), Turin (Italy), Västerås (Sweden), Venice (Italy), Vienna (Austria), Warsaw (Poland) and Yeovilton (England)

Asia – Amman (Jordan), Aqaba (Jordan), Bahrain, Bali (Indonesia), Bangkok (Thailand), Beijing (China), Chennai (India), Colombo (Sri Lanka), Dhahran (Saudi Arabia), Delhi (India), Hong Kong, Jakarta (Indonesia), Jeddah (Saudi Arabia), Kolkata (India), Kuala Lumpur (Malaysia), Kuwait, Mumbai (India), Riyadh (Saudi Arabia), Singapore, Tashkent (Uzbekistan) and Tel Aviv (Israel)

G-BOAF is approaching Heathrow on 24 October 2003, behind G-BOAE and in front of G-BOAG, after flying its final passenger-carrying flight. It was the last Concorde to fly when it was delivered to Filton, via the Bay of Biscay, on 26 November 2003. (Via *Aeroplane*)

The first Concorde to be delivered to BA in January 1974, G-BOAA is pictured whilst flying the Braniff routes as G-N94AA during 1979. It is sporting the original single 'British' Negus & Negus-designed livery. (Martyn Chorlton)

Concorde gave BA faultless service during its 27 years with the airline on almost 50,000 flights, carrying 2.5 million passengers at supersonic speed. When the fleet was grounded in 2000, BA embraced the changes, modifications and upgrades required to get the aircraft back in the air. With all of the fleet on the ground at the same time, the opportunity to relaunch the aircraft with a new 'Union Flag' livery and new interiors was taken. The first BA passenger-carrying flight took place on that infamous day, 11 September 2001, the aircraft touching down at JFK just before the first airliner plunged into the World Trade Center. This really was the beginning of the end for Concorde and the air travel industry would never be the same again.

While BA was still managing to make a profit, Air France had been on the back foot since the Paris accident and the British carrier was not prepared to shoulder the financial responsibility of the aircraft on its own. Air France withdrew its aircraft earlier than planned while BA stuck to its plan, and, during October 2003, its aircraft began a series of farewell tours that took in Canada, the US and various locations around Britain before the final three aircraft brought the commercial days of Concorde to an end at Heathrow on 24 October 2003.

THE BRITISH AIRWAYS FLEET – 1976–2003	
G-BOAA	Delivered to BA 14 January 1976; retired 12 August 2000; 22,768hrs 56mins
G-BOAB	Delivered to BA 30 September 1976; retired 15 August 2000; 22,296hrs 55mins
G-BOAC	Delivered to BA 13 February 1976; retired 31 October 2003; 22,260hrs 11mins
G-BOAD	Delivered to BA 6 December 1976; retired 10 November 2003; 23,397hrs 25mins
G-BOAE	Delivered to BA 20 July 1977; retired 17 November 2003; 23,376hrs 7mins
G-BOAF	Delivered to BA 9 June 1980; retired 26 November 2003; 18,257hrs
G-BOAG	Delivered to BA 6 February 1980; retired 5 November 2003; 16,239hrs 27mins

G-BOAG flew its last commercial flight from JFK on 24 October 2003; it is pictured on final approach to Heathrow. (Via François Prins)

Dramatic view of G-BOAD from the back seat of a Red Arrows Hawk T.1, on 4 June 2002, during the Queen's Jubilee Flypast. Civil Aviation Authority (CAA) chief test pilot Jock Reid and Captain Mike Bannister were at the controls. (Martyn Chorlton)

Chapter 7

The Passenger-Carrying Fleet

The first production Concorde

It is slightly ironic that the first production Concorde was destined to become the most well-known of all for all the wrong reasons. The incident that would claim it, all 109 passengers on board and four on the ground has sadly cast a shadow over this amazing aircraft that has proved to be very hard to lift. However, as evidence to explain exactly what occurred on that fateful day has been revealed, the aircraft has been exonerated of all blame and it was concluded that a classic combination of errors by man rather than machine, caused the disaster.

First flown on 31 January 1975 from Toulouse as F-WTSC, registered to Aérospatiale, the Concorde was reregistered as F-BTSC, again by Aérospatiale, on 28 May 1975. The aircraft was not leased to Air France until 6 January 1975, having spent the remainder of the previous year carrying various route proving flights. By late 1976, more Concordes were delivered to Air France and F-BTSC was returned to Aérospatiale on 8 December 1976. During 1977, the airliner embarked on a Middle East sales tour, where only Iran showed a serious interest to purchase. In the 1979, F-BTSC took on the starring role in disaster film *The Concorde: Airport '79*, before being re-leased to Air France on 11 June 1979. Twelve months later, the airliner was upgraded from a Type 100 to a Type 101, and, on 23 October 1980, Air France purchased F-BTSC outright for the princely sum of one franc!

Captured on approach to Charles de Gaulle in September 1999, only a few weeks before the aircraft was returned to service after a long and expensive 'D' check. (Manuel Negrerie)

CONCORDE 100 (LATER 101) (S/N 203)

MAIDEN FLIGHT: 31 January 1975 from Toulouse

REGISTRATION HISTORY: First registered as F-WTSC to Aérospatiale; reregistered as F-BTSC by Aérospatiale 28 May 1975; leased to Air France 6 January 1976; returned to Aérospatiale 8 December 1976; re-leased to Air France 11 June 1979; converted to Type 101 June 1980; purchased by Air France 23 October 1980

TOTAL FLYING HOURS: 11,989hrs

LANDINGS: 3,978

FINAL FLIGHT: July 25, 2000 from Charles de Gaulle Airport; crashed La Patte d'Oie, Gonesse, France

CURRENT LOCATION: Remains at Le Bourget

Along with F-BVFD, the Concorde was placed into storage from late 1982 when Air France's fleet went through a particularly unprofitable period and was not reintroduced to service until 28 April 1986 to cover the routes of Concordes that were grounded due to engineering checks. The airliner continued in service until June 1998 when the airframe was due to undergo an expensive and time consuming 'D' check, which involved ultrasonic, radiographic and visual checks. Serious corrosion was found, which resulted in the keel beam having to be replaced at a cost of £4m. After 60,000-man hours and three weeks of ground testing, followed by two flight tests, F-BTSC was back in service from 1 November 1999.

At 1442hrs, on 25 July 2000, with Capt Christian Marty at the controls, 1st Officer Jean Marcot in the co-pilots seat and flight engineer Gilles Jardinaud sitting behind, F-BTSC began to roll down Paris Charles de Gaulle's Runway 26 Right, with 100 passengers and six cabin crew on board. Two minutes later, F-BTSC crashed into a hotel at La Patte d'Oie in Gonesse killing all 109 on board and four on the ground. This was the first and last loss of a Concorde.

In memory of BOAC

The very first British-built production Concorde was the first of five that were originally ordered by BOAC on 28 July 1972. Even though it was destined to be slightly out of sequence, this aircraft was appropriately registered as G-BOAC by BAC Ltd on 3 April 1974, despite the fact BOAC had ceased to exist just three days earlier, having merged with BEA to form BA.

First flown on 27 February 1975, G-BOAC received its CoA on 30 June, and from 7 July, began a series of endurance test flights taking in London, Bahrain, Bombay, Kuala Lumpur, Singapore, Melbourne, Beirut, Gander and Damascus. G-BOAC carried out four Atlantic crossings in a single day on 1 September 1975, when the Concorde flew from London to Gander and back, twice! With 141 flights already to its credit, the aircraft was refurbished and delivered to BA on 16 February 1975 to become the second Concorde in the fleet, although it would always be treated as the flag ship. The aircraft was chosen to carry out the first flight to Washington on 26 May 1976. Reregistered as G-N81AC/N81AC whilst flying routes for Braniff Airways ('interchange operation') from 5 January 1979, the aircraft was reregistered back as G-BOAC by August 1980.

G-BOAC recorded the highest ground speed of a commercial airliner in service on 19 December 1985 at an eye-watering 1,488mph. The Concorde enjoyed a trouble-free period of operations until the aircraft hit the headlines on 24 May 1998, when the airliner suffered a separation of the number three port elevon. The negative headlines continued on 8 October, when G-BOAC suffered a lower rudder wedge failure, which, unlike the elevon, was not an original component, as they had been replaced on all of the BA fleet just four years earlier. Concorde's troubles did not go away, and, following the loss

CONCORDE 102 (S/N 204)

MAIDEN FLIGHT: 27 February 1975 from Filton

REGISTRATION HISTORY: First registered as G-BOAC 3 April 1974 to BAC Ltd; delivered to BA 13 February 1976; reregistered as G-N81AC/N81AC by BA/Braniff Airways 5 January 1979; reregistered as G-BOAC by BA on 11 August 1980; de-registered 4 May 2004

TOTAL SUPERSONIC FLIGHTS: 6,761

TOTAL FLYING HOURS: 22,260hrs 11mins

LANDINGS: 7,730

FINAL FLIGHT: 31 October 2003, Heathrow to Manchester

CURRENT LOCATION: Manchester Airport

of F-BTSC, the type's CoA was withdrawn on 15 August 2000. G-BOAC was literally on the end of the runway at Heathrow, just about to depart for New York, when the news came through and the airliner was ordered back to the stand.

Modification work took time, but, once the authorities were happy, G-BOAC was back in the air on 11 July 2002, after being grounded for 23 months. G-BOAC settled in to flying the BA001/002 service to New York from 23 July, and it looked like the good old days had returned. However, the end was getting close for Concorde, but G-BOAC, with Capt Les Brodie at the controls, had the privilege of flying to Barbados to return the Queen to Britain after her demanding Jubilee tour. On 31 October 2003, G-BOAC made its final flight from Heathrow to Manchester, where today the Concorde is protected from the elements in 'glass hangar' positioned on the edge of the viewing park.

British Airways future flagship, G-BOAC, on the tarmac at Melbourne, after one of many proving flights. (Via *Aeroplane*)

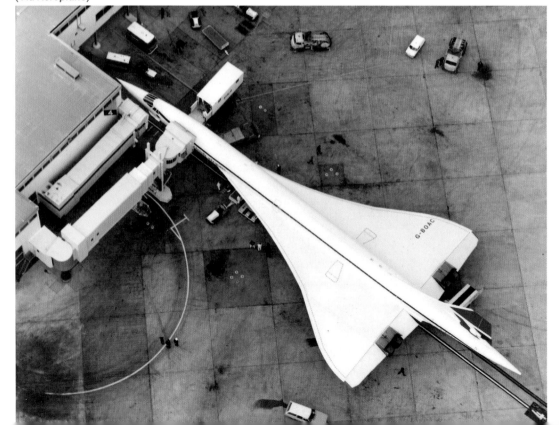

CONCORDE 101 (S/N 205)

MAIDEN FLIGHT: 27 October 1975 from Toulouse

REGISTRATION HISTORY: First registered as F-BVFA to Air France; delivered to Air France 19 December 1975; reregistered as N94FA by Air France/Braniff Airways 12 January 1979; reregistered to Air France as F-BVFA 1 June 1980

TOTAL FLYING HOURS: 17,824hrs

TOTAL SUPERSONIC CYCLES: 5,504

LANDINGS: 6,780

FINAL PASSENGER FLIGHT: 30 May 2003, (AF001) JFK to Charles De Gaulle

FINAL FLIGHT: 12 June 2003, (AF4386) Charles de Gaulle to Dulles

CURRENT LOCATION: Smithsonian Institution National Air and Space Museum's Steven F Udvar-Hazy Center, Dulles, Washington DC

Launching Air France services to the Americas

First flown from Toulouse on 27 October 1975, F-BVFA joined Air France in 1976 and, later that same year, launched Air France's service to Rio, Washington and New York. One of Air France's hard-working fleet, F-BVFA, steadily built up its flying hours and was one of several aircraft that flew the Braniff Airways service in 1979 and early 1980, being reregistered as N94FA during this period. The aircraft stayed out of the limelight until 1988, when it set a new round-the-world, record-breaking time of 41hrs 27mins.

On 25 February 2003, F-BVFA was the first Air France Concorde to suffer from rudder delamination, though up to this time several BA Concordes had already experienced the problem. The flying hours matched that of the BA aircraft that first suffered from the problem back in the late 1980s. A 50cm section of the lower rudder bottom wedge was found by inspectors to be missing and a 130cm section of the lower rudder's upper wedge had gone as well.

Concorde F-BVFA in 'Euro-white' livery, which was introduced in the late 1970s and remained until the type's retirement. The aircraft takes pride of place in the Smithsonian Institution National Air and Space Museum's Steven F. Udvar-Hazy Center, Dulles, Washington DC. (Martyn Chorlton)

F-BVFA continued in service until 30 May 2003, and, in an agreement that was made back in the 1990s, Air France donated the aircraft to the Smithsonian Institution National Air and Space Museum's Steven F. Udvar-Hazy Center at Dulles on 12 June 2003.

British Airways' first Concorde

The first of seven Concordes that were destined to serve with BA was delivered to the airline on 14 January 1976, after a 42-minute flight from Fairford to Heathrow. Just seven days later, G-BOAA flew the first service to Bahrain with Capt Norman Todd at the controls, and, on 22 November 1977, it also made the inaugural flight to New York, this time in the hands of Capt Brian Walpole.

CONCORDE 102 (S/N 206)
MAIDEN FLIGHT: 5 November 1975 from Filton
REGISTRATION HISTORY: First registered as G-BOAA 3 March 1974 to BAC Ltd; delivered to BA 14 January 1976; reregistered G-N94AA/N94AA by BA/Braniff Airways 12 January 1979; reregistered G-BOAA by BA 28 July 1980; de-registered 4 May 2004
TOTAL FLYING HOURS: 22,768hrs 56mins
TOTAL SUPERSONIC FLYING HOURS: 6,842 (Cycles)
LANDINGS: 8,064
FINAL FLIGHT: 12 August 2000, (BA002) JFK to Heathrow
CURRENT LOCATION: National Museum of Flight, East Fortune (delivered 8–19 April 2004)

G-BOAA is pictured here in 1976, not long after joining BA on 14 January. Its unplanned retirement on 12 August 2000 brought to an end a 24-year flying career, which totalled 22,768 flying hours. (Martyn Chorlton)

G-BOAA was the first Concorde to reach 12,000 flying hours in April 1988, at which point, the airframe was subjected to a major maintenance check, which revealed that the aircraft was in fine order and was cleared to fly into the 21st century. The aircraft joined a Spitfire over Dover on 6 June 1990 to celebrate the 50th Anniversary of the Battle of Britain. Another well-publicised event in which G-BOAA was involved was on 2 June 1996 when, in company with the Red Arrows, the airliner helped to celebrate the 50th Anniversary of Heathrow Airport.

In 1993, G-BOAA was fitted with a new rudder at a cost of £1m but, following the grounding of all Concordes after the Paris crash, it was never modified, and, without ceremony, its final flight took place from New York to Heathrow on 12 August 2000. G-BOAA languished at Heathrow until early 2004 when it was allocated, for preservation, to the National Museum of Flight at East Fortune in Scotland. It was rather crudely dismantled (its wings were cut rather than dismantled at the manufacturer's joints), transported by road to the River Thames and loaded onto a barge. G-BOAA then travelled along the east of coast of Britain and was unloaded at Torness Power Station to make its final 14-mile-long journey via the A1 to the Museum of Flight.

Shoulder to shoulder with the Tu-144

First flown from Toulouse on 6 March 1976, F-BVFB was in service with Air France just over four weeks later. One of the four Air France Concordes to fly for Braniff in 1979 and 1980, F-BVFB continued in regular, but not demanding, use until June 1990. Due to this lack of utilisation, F-BVFB was placed into storage until May 1997, because the aircraft was the closest of the Air France fleet to the 12,000hr 'D' check. Work began in April 1996 to prepare F-BVFB to return to service to replace F-BVFC, which was approaching its own 'D' check.

Grounded with the rest of the fleet following the Paris crash, F-BVFB was flown to Istres on 26 January 2001 where it was subjected to a number of tests and trials by an investigative team until 3 February. On 24 August, F-BVFB became the first Air France Concorde to fly again, following the installation of post-crash modifications; during the test flight, the airliner broke Mach 1. An assessment flight was carried out to New York and back in October, followed by normal resumption of services.

F-BVFB flew its final passenger-carrying flight on 31 May 2003 and, on 24 June, the final flight took place from Charles de Gaulle to Karlsruhe for delivery by road to the excellent Technik Museum Sinsheim in Sinsheim, Germany. The airliner is dramatically posed in a nose up attitude, several feet above the ground alongside Tu-144 77112, positioned in a similar 'flying' display since it arrived in 2001. Both airliners are accessible via spiral staircases.

CONCORDE 101 (S/N 207)

MAIDEN FLIGHT: 6 March 1976 from Toulouse

REGISTRATION HISTORY: First registered as F-BVFB to Air France; delivered to Air France 8 April 1976; reregistered as N94FB by Air France/Braniff Airways 12 January 1979; reregistered to Air France as F-BVFB 1 June 1980

TOTAL FLYING HOURS: 14,771hrs

TOTAL CYCLES: 4,791

LANDINGS: 5,473

FINAL PASSENGER FLIGHT: 31 May 2003, (AF4332) Charles De Gaulle charter

FINAL FLIGHT: 24 June 2003, (AF4406) Charles de Gaulle to Karlsruhe Baden-Baden

CURRENT LOCATION: Technik Museum Sinsheim, Germany

The dramatically displayed F-BVFB, which, along with several other airliners, including a Tu-144, is presented in flight configuration. (Martyn Chorlton)

'Alpha-Bravo'

One of the more well-known Concordes, thanks to its long 'static' association with Heathrow Airport, G-BOAB made its maiden flight on 18 May 1976. On this first flight from Fairford, BAC test pilot, Capt Eddie McNamara flew the aircraft for 3hrs 32mins, reaching a speed of Mach 2.05 at a height of 63,500ft. A further 12 test flights were carried out before the aircraft became the third Concorde to be delivered to BA on 14 January 1976. During the delivery flight, which lasted 1hr 20mins, the BA crew, Capt Tony Meadows and Capt Brian Walpole carried out touch and goes at Gatwick Airport, before arriving at Heathrow.

CONCORDE 102 (S/N 208)

MAIDEN FLIGHT: 18 May 1976 from Filton

REGISTRATION HISTORY: First registered as G-BOAB 3 April 1974 to BAC Ltd; delivered to BA 30 September 1976; reregistered G-N94AB/N94AB by BA/Braniff Airways 12 January 1979; reregistered G-BOAB by BA 17 September 1980; de-registered 4 May 2004

TOTAL FLYING HOURS: 22,296hrs 55mins

TOTAL SUPERSONIC CYCLES: 6,688

LANDINGS: 7,810

FINAL FLIGHT: 15 August 2000, (BA002P) JFK to Heathrow

CURRENT LOCATION: Heathrow Airport

On 11 September 1984, G-BOAB set a new distance record for an airliner when it flew from Washington to Nice, a distance of 4,565 miles. On 16 November, the airliner flew the first charter service from London to Seattle via New York.

G-BOAB made its final flight, although no one knew it at the time, from JFK to Heathrow on 15 August 2000, in the hands of Capt Les Brodie. The aircraft was being prepared for its inter-check and would have been the sixth Concorde to return to service from the Paris crash, but BA only needed five.

While all of its fellow aircraft were either flown out or dismantled and despatched to museums around the world, G-BOAB stayed put at Heathrow and was still owned by BA. Various plans for

G-BOAD, in 1979, when it was flying for Braniff as G-N94AD and displaying Singapore Airlines livery; the colours were only on the port side of the fuselage. (Martyn Chorlton)

the aircraft included use as a gate guardian and even as an exhibit hanging from the new Terminal 5 ceiling. Nothing came to fruition, and BA decided to gift the aircraft to British Airports Authority (BAA), the owners of Heathrow airport, in 21 January 2004, the 28th anniversary of Concorde's entry into service. The gift was under the proviso that G-BOAB would remain at Heathrow and, from then on, the aircraft was parked not far from Runway 26, in a position nicknamed 'Point Rocket' by the employees of the airport. However, on 10 May 2006, G-BOAB was towed away from 'Point Rocket' and placed out of sight in BA's old engine test area, when the Spanish company Ferrovial took over BAA. Today, G-BOAB is back in public view not far from the end of Runway 27, a good move for BA, as the old engine test area has since been demolished to make room for parking long-haul aircraft during the winter.

The last Air France Concorde to fly

After making its first flight from Toulouse on 9 July 1976, F-BVFC joined Air France on 3 August. Other than taking part in the Braniff co-operation, F-BVFC had an uneventful career, which was only interrupted by the 12,000hr 'D' check between March 1997 and May 1998. It was caught on the ground in New York when the CoA was withdrawn on 16 August 2000 and did not return to Paris until 21 September.

F-BVFC carried out its final flight on 27 June 2003 when it was initially retired to the Airbus Factory at Toulouse. During the flight, the captain took one last opportunity to fly supersonic and carried out a go around before it landed for the final time.

CONCORDE 101 (S/N 209)
MAIDEN FLIGHT: 9 July 1976 from Toulouse
REGISTRATION HISTORY: First registered as F-BVFC to Air France; delivered to Air France 3 August 1976; reregistered as N94FC by Air France/Braniff Airways 12 January 1979; reregistered to Air France as F-BVFC 1 June 1980
TOTAL FLYING HOURS: 14,332hrs
TOTAL SUPERSONIC FLIGHTS: 4,200
LANDINGS: 4,358
FINAL FLIGHT: 27 June 2003, (AF6903) Charles de Gaulle to Toulouse
CURRENT LOCATION: Musée Aeroscopia, Toulouse

Embraced by the 'Big Apple'

It seems ironic that an aircraft that was banned from serving its main airport over three decades ago is now embraced by New York City and has become one of its most popular visitor attractions. G-BOAD was never a stranger to New York once the restrictions had been lifted, and the aircraft first joined BA on 6 December 1976.

The airliner was destined to become the only BA Concorde to sport the livery of another airline when, in 1977, the port side of the fuselage was repainted in Singapore Airlines' colours. A joint service was announced by the two airlines in October, with a service commencing in December from London to Singapore, via Bahrain. G-BOAD only flew three flights before the Malaysian government objected to Concorde flying over its territory. G-BOAD resumed the service in January 1979, but the route was abandoned for good in November 1980, as it was proving to be uneconomical.

Concorde G-BOAG approaching Heathrow's Runway 27 to land on 24 October 2003, after completing its final passenger-carrying flight from New York. (Martyn Chorlton)

On 7 February 1996, G-BOAD carried out the world's fastest transatlantic airliner flight from JFK to Heathrow in just 2hrs 52mins 59secs, from take-off to landing, aided by a 175mph tailwind; a record that will stand for the foreseeable future!

The year 2002 was busy for G-BOAD, which was back in service after its modification programme was completed on 29 January. On 10 February, normal services from Heathrow to New York were resumed and, on 4 June, G-BOAD took part in one of the final, memorable formation flypasts, in company with the Red Arrows for the Queen's Golden Jubilee.

On 8 October 2003, G-BOAD took part in a farewell tour that included a visit to Boston, and, stamping its final authority as being the fastest Concorde in the BA fleet, the flight from east to west was performed in a record time of 3hrs 5mins 34secs. Concorde still had one more final visit to make to the US, but this time it would not be coming home. On 10 November 2003, G-BOAD made its final crossing of the Atlantic to JFK where it was decommissioned in preparation for display at the Intrepid Sea, Air and Space Museum on the USS *Intrepid*, New York.

CONCORDE 102 (S/N 210)

MAIDEN FLIGHT: 25 August 1976 from Filton

REGISTRATION HISTORY: First registered as G-BOAD to BAC; delivered to BA 6 Decmeber 1976; reregistered as G-N94AD/N94AD by BA/Braniff Airways 5 January 1979; reregistered to BA as G-BOAD 19 June 1980; de-registered 4 May 2004

TOTAL FLYING HOURS: 23,397hrs 25mins

TOTAL SUPERSONIC FLIGHTS: 7,010

LANDINGS: 8,406

FINAL FLIGHT: 10 November 2003, Heathrow to JFK

CURRENT LOCATION: Intrepid Sea, Air and Space Museum, New York

Short career and an undignified end

Delivered to Air France on 26 March 1977, F-BVFD was destined to have the shortest commercial career of all the passenger-carrying Concordes through no fault of its own. It had only been in service for a few months when the Concorde suffered a heavy landing at Dakar in November 1977. Landed at 14ft/sec rather than the recommended ten, this was enough to crush the rear tail bumper wheel and put years' worth of strain on the airframe. F-BVFD was retired and placed into storage after carrying out what was to be its last flight on 27 May 1982.

With just 5,814hrs on the airframe, F-BVFD remained in storage at Charles de Gaulle until 1994, when Air France decided to break it up because of serious corrosion issues. Only the nose assembly was sold to a US collector on 16 March 1995 for 300,000 French francs (€45,730), while the remainder of the aircraft was broken up and stored at Dugny, where it lies to this day.

CONCORDE 101 (S/N 211)
MAIDEN FLIGHT: 10 February 1977 from Toulouse
REGISTRATION HISTORY: First registered as F-BVFD to Air France; delivered to Air France 26 March 1977; reregistered as N94FD by Air France/Braniff Airways 12 January 1979; reregistered to Air France as F-BVFD 1 June 1980
TOTAL FLYING HOURS: 5,814hrs
TOTAL SUPERSONIC FLIGHTS: 1,807
LANDINGS: 1,929
FINAL FLIGHT: 27 May 1982
CURRENT LOCATION: remains at Dugny

'Caribbean Queen'

G-BOAE first flew from Filton on 17 March 1977 and was delivered to BA on 20 July. The aircraft settled into many years of regular service plying its trade across the Atlantic, but it was not until 1 July 1999 that G-BOAE began to take its share of the limelight. On that day, it joined the Red Arrows for a formation flypast over Edinburgh and Glasgow in celebration of the opening of the Scottish Parliament. Just two days before all Concordes were due to be grounded because of the Paris air crash, cracks were found in G-BOAE's wings on 23 July 2000. They were found not to be serious and, once repaired, G-BOAE was ready to return to the air by late 2001.

CONCORDE 102 (S/N 212)
MAIDEN FLIGHT: 17 March 1977 from Filton
REGISTRATION HISTORY: First registered as G-BOAE 9 May 1975 to BAC Ltd; delivered to BA 20 July 1977; reregistered G-N94AE/N94AE by BA/Braniff Airways 5 January 1979; reregistered G-BOAE by BA 1 July 1980; de-registered 4 May 2004
TOTAL FLYING HOURS: 23,376hrs 7mins
TOTAL SUPERSONIC CYCLES: 7,003
LANDINGS: 8,383
FINAL FLIGHT: 17 November 2003, Heathrow to Grantley Adams Airport, Barbados
CURRENT LOCATION: Grantley Adams Airport, Barbados

On 7 November 2001, G-BOAE became the first BA Concorde to fly passengers again in a flight from Heathrow to New York. G-BOAE also flew on the final day of Concorde operations on 24 October 2003, when, in the hands of Capt Andy Baillie and Les Brodie, the aircraft joined G-BOAF and G-BOAG for a low circuit of London before all three landed back at Heathrow after just after 1600hrs.

Its final flight was on 17 November 2003, when it was delivered to Grantley Adams Airport in Barbados, where G-BOAE is now displayed in the Barbados Concorde Experience on the edge of the airport.

Fastest around the world

First flown on 26 June 1978, F-BTSD was leased by Air France on and off until the aircraft was purchased outright on 23 October 1980. F-BTSD stayed out of the limelight until 12–13 October 1992, when the airliner set a new 'westbound around the world' record in a time of 32hrs 49mins 3secs. The flight departed from Lisbon with refuelling points at Santo Domingo, Acapulco, Honolulu, Guam (Anderson AFB), Bangkok and Bahrain before landing back at Lisbon. The flight was a charter by Concorde Spirit Tours (US) to commemorate the 500th anniversary of Columbus' discovery of the New World.

The same charter company used F-BTSD again on 15–16 August 1995, when the airliner set a new 'eastbound around the world' record in just 31hrs 27min 49secs. This flight departed from JFK via Toulouse, Dubai, Bangkok, Guam, Honolulu, Acapulco and back to New York.

In 1996, F-BTSD was chosen to help promote Pepsi as part of a US$500m rebranding exercise. As a result, the aircraft was repainted dark blue, which posed an initial problem because the reason why Concorde was painted white was to disperse heat, especially whilst travelling at Mach 2. The aircraft was only certified to fly at twice the speed of sound in white, and a compromise was reached where the wings would remain white, and the aircraft was not to be flown at Mach 2 for more than 20 minutes. No restrictions were applied below Mach 1.7, but the speed was irrelevant, as Air France was not planning on using the aircraft for any schedule flights to New York at the time.

After the Paris air crash, F-BTSD carried out trials of a new Michelin tyre at Istres before it returned to service. The aircraft carried out its final passenger flight on 31 May 2003 and, on 14 June, was delivered from Charles to Gaulle to Paris Le Bourget, where today, it is preserved in excellent order at the Air and Space Museum. Thanks to the attention showered on this aircraft by former Air France Concorde engineer Alexandra Jolivet, F-BTSD is as close to a fully airworthy aircraft as a museum piece can be, with all of its hydraulics systems and electrics still functioning and even the nose and visor are still in working order.

CONCORDE 101 (S/N 213)

MAIDEN FLIGHT: 26 June 1978 from Toulouse

REGISTRATION HISTORY: First registered as F-WJAM to Aérospatiale; reregistered as F-BTSD by Aérospatiale; leased to Air France 18 September 1978; reregistered as N94SD by Air France/Braniff Airways 12 January 1979; reregistered as F-BTSD and returned to Aérospatiale 12 March 1979; leased to Air France 9 May 1980; purchased by Air France 23 October 1980

TOTAL FLYING HOURS: 12,974hrs

TOTAL SUPERSONIC CYCLES: 3,672

LANDINGS: 5,135

FINAL PASSENGER FLIGHT: 31 May 2003, (AF001) JFK to Charles de Gaulle

FINAL FLIGHT: 14 June 2003, (AF380Y) Charles de Gaulle to Le Bourget

CURRENT LOCATION: Musée de l'Air et de l'Espace, Le Bourget, Paris

---

Kilo-Whiskey to Alpha-Golf

Registered as G-BFKW in January 1978 by British Aerospace, this Concorde made its maiden flight on 21 April. The aircraft was held in storage at Filton until it was loaned to BA to cover for G-BOAC, which was under repair. This initial period of service with BA came to a premature end on 26 April 1980, when the aircraft had to turn back to Heathrow having suffered an intake ramp failure at Mach 2. This was found to have been caused by water that had contaminated the hydraulic system. This was repaired at a cost of £1m, and the aircraft re-entered BA service permanently in February 1981 and was reregistered as G-BOAG. BA suffered a spares shortage during the early 1980s and partly to solve this, G-BOAG was grounded to keep the rest of the fleet in the air until 1984, when G-BBDG took over as the chief 'hangar queen'.

G-BOAG was brought back into service in 1985 and, on 25 April, it was the first BA Concorde to sport the new Landor livery, which timed with the floatation of the airline on the London Stock Exchange. The aircraft was also the star of the show at RIAT at RAF Fairford, when it carried out a flypast with the Red Arrows.

From May 1996, G-BOAG underwent a major refurbishment programme, inside and out and, in December 1996, was the last of the fleet to be repainted in the final Union Flag livery. Post Paris

CONCORDE 102 (S/N 214)
MAIDEN FLIGHT: 21 April 1978 from Filton
REGISTRATION HISTORY: First registered as G-BFKW 27 January 1978 to British Aerospace; delivered to BA 6 February 1980; reregistered G-BOAG by BA 9 February 1981; de-registered 4 May 2004
TOTAL FLYING HOURS: 16,239hrs 27mins
TOTAL SUPERSONIC CYCLES: 5,066
LANDINGS: 5,633
FINAL FLIGHT: 5 November 2003, JFK to Seattle
CURRENT LOCATION: Museum of Flight, Seattle, Washington

F-BVFF was the first Air France Concorde to fly around the world on a charter flight. (Manuel Negrerie)

air crash, it was the third BA Concorde to be modified and put back into service. G-BOAG began its contribution to the Concorde farewell tour on 1 October 2003 with a visit to Toronto. From there, the North American tour began, concluding in Washington on 14 October. On 22 October, the aircraft visited Manchester and, two days later, carried out its final flight from New York, joining G-BOAE and G-BOAF for a low circuit of the capital before touching down at Heathrow for the final time.

On 3 November 2003, G-BOAG left Heathrow bound for New York on the first stage of its journey into retirement at the Museum of Flight, Seattle, Washington. On 5 November, it left JFK, having been given special permission fly supersonic, which resulted in a new speed record from the east to the west of North America.

First around the world

Originally registered as F-WJAN, this aircraft flew for the first time on 26 December 1978 and was delivered to Air France on 23 October 1980. Reregistered as F-BVFF the same day, the airliner went on to become the first Air France Concorde to fly around the world on a charter flight and would fly a further 11 circumnavigations before its retirement.

Its final charter flight was carried out on 11 June 2000, when it was withdrawn for planned maintenance work. F-BVFF donated several of its components to F-BTSD, which was going through its 'D' check at the same time and, once the latter was back in service, work would begin again to return F-BVFF to the air. Work only began on F-BVFF in April 2002, and the modifications were only two-thirds complete when Air France announced that it would soon be ending Concorde services. Work was brought to an abrupt halt and the aircraft was made presentable and placed on display on three supporting legs in the middle of Paris Charles de Gaulle airport. Pointing towards New York, the aircraft is not accessible but can be viewed by the general public.

CONCORDE 101 (S/N 215)

MAIDEN FLIGHT: 26 December 1978 from Toulouse

REGISTRATION HISTORY: First registered as F-WJAN to Aérospatiale; delivered to Air France 23 October 1980 and reregistered as F-BVFF the same day

TOTAL FLYING HOURS: 12,421hrs

TOTAL SUPERSONIC CYCLES: 3,734

LANDINGS: 4,259

FINAL FLIGHT: 11 June 2000, (AF4586) charter flight

CURRENT LOCATION: Charles de Gaulle, Paris

Filton's own

There has been much speculation as to how much, or little, BA and Air France paid for some of their Concordes, especially the final production aircraft (guesses range from £1 to £1000). Whatever the sum that may have been paid, British Aerospace would have been glad to have moved the aircraft on to the charge of BA.

First registered as G-BFKX in January 1978, the aircraft did not make its maiden flight from Filton until 20 April 1979. By the end of the year, the Concorde was reregistered as G-BOAF and leased to BA before the aircraft was 'purchased' and delivery took place in June 1980. It is a fact BA did spend £1m on its own 'Buyer Furnished' equipment, which included radios, navigation aids, galleys and seats.

G-BOAF achieved a number of firsts during its career, not all were notable, including the moment when it became the first Concorde to suffer rudder separation failure during a flight from Christchurch to Sydney on 12 April 1989. In 2001, G-BOAF was the first BA Concorde to be refitted with leather seats and, in the same year, it was the first back in the air following the Paris crash. The modification programme included several upgrades but most importantly were the installation Kevlar fuel tank

G-BOAF, which first flew from Filton on 20 April 1979, returns for good on 26 November 2003. (Martyn Chorlton)

liners and of new, strengthened electrical wiring around the main undercarriage. On 17 July 2001, the first 'return to flight' upgrades were successfully trialled in the air and, on 22 October, a final operational assessment flight was performed with a return flight to New York. On 1 December, the aircraft began a weekly service to Barbados.

G-BOAF flew its final passenger-carrying flight on 24 October 2003, which was a short supersonic loop over the Atlantic, before joining G-BOAE and G-BOAG for a final pass over London. It was not until 30 October that BA confirmed that G-BOAF would be retired to Filton. This final flight, which was the last flown by all Concordes, was carried out on 26 November from Heathrow, went via the Bay of Biscay and was followed by a low pass over the Clifton suspension bridge before landing at its spiritual home of Filton.

After being fully decommissioned, G-BOAF was placed in open storage over the winter while a new display area was prepared on the southern side of the airfield. It was towed to this location on 20 March 2003, and, once the visitor centre was completed, G-BOAF was opened to the public on 18 August 2004.

CONCORDE 102 (S/N 216)

MAIDEN FLIGHT: 20 April 1979 from Filton

REGISTRATION HISTORY: First registered as G-BFKX 27 January 1978 to British Aerospace; reregistered G-N94AF/G-BOAF by British Aerospace 14 December 1979; delivered to BA 8 June 1980; reregistered G-BOAF by BA 12 June 1980; de-registered 4 May 2004

TOTAL FLYING HOURS: 18,257hrs

TOTAL SUPERSONIC CYCLES: 5,639

LANDINGS: 6,045

FINAL FLIGHT: 26 November 2003, Heathrow to Filton

CURRENT LOCATION: Filton

TECH INFO PRODUCTION 101/102

ENGINES: Four 32,520lb (dry), 38,050lb (reheat) Bristol Siddeley/SNECMA Olympus 593-3B Mk 610-14-28 turbojets

LENGTH: 203ft 9in (61.10m)

WINGSPAN: 83ft 10in (25.55m)

HEIGHT: 40ft (12.2m)

FUSELAGE INTERNAL LENGTH: 129ft (39.32m)

FUSELAGE MAX INTERNAL WIDTH: 8ft 7½in (2.62m)

FUSELAGE MAX INTERNAL HEIGHT: 6ft 5in (1.95m)

MAX TAKE-OFF WEIGHT: 400,000lb

MAX LANDING WEIGHT: 245,000lb

PASSENGERS: 100 to 131

MAX SPEED: Mach 2.2

INITIAL CLIMB RATE: 5,000ft/min

CEILING: 60,000ft

RANGE: 3,550 miles with max fuel and 3,360 miles with max payload

CONCORDE FACTS AND FIGURES

British Airways flew Concorde for just under 50,000 flights

2.5 million passengers flew supersonically on British Airways Concordes

220kts (250mph) was Concorde's take off speed

2hrs 52mins 59secs was the fastest transatlantic crossing time achieved on 7 February 1996 by G-BOAD, assisted by a 175mph tailwind

29hrs 59mins was the time it took a BA Concorde to fly around the world (28,238 miles) in November 1986

6-10 inches was the amount the airframe stretched during supersonic flight

Jose Maria Olazabal performed the longest golf putt at 9.232 miles whilst travelling at 1,270mph in 1999.

US astronauts are more common than BA Concorde pilots!

£6,636 was the standard return fare from London to New York

More than one million bottles of champagne have been consumed on Concorde passenger flights

15.8 passenger miles per gallon was all Concorde could achieve compared to a DC-10, which returned 53.6 passenger miles per gallon

Two tonnes of fuel were consumed by the aircraft before it reached the end of the runway

300–400°C was the temperature of the carbon brakes of Concorde after a normal landing

G-BOAG established a new New York City to Seattle (east to west) record of 3hrs 55mins 12secs on 5 November 2003 – its final flight

6,000 gallons of fuel per hour were consumed during a typical flight from London to New York

At Mach 2, the temperature of the nose and trailing edges reach 127°C

80 per cent of Concorde passengers were male and 43 per cent were either managing directors or senior managers; their average age was 43

Barbara Hamer became Concorde's first female pilot in 1993

Prince Philip was the first royal to fly in Concorde in January 1972

Concorde 001 F-WTSS, which flew for the first time at 1540hrs on 2 March 1969 from Toulouse. This historic event was carried out by Aérospatiale test pilot André Turcat (right), with Jacques Guignard as co-pilot (second from right), Michel Retief as the flight engineer and three flight test observers. (Airbus Group)

Brian Trubshaw puts Concorde 002 G-BSST through its paces at Farnborough on 1 September 1970; a few days later, the aircraft landed at Heathrow for the first time. (*Aeroplane*)

Concorde's VIP visitors at Fairford, Gloucestershire. Standing beneath the now familiar profile of the Anglo-French project Concorde are (from left) John Davis, British Secretary for Trade and Industry; Brian Trubshaw, chief test pilot for Concorde 002; and Lord Carrington, Britain's Minister of Aviation. They are pictured before Trubshaw took them on a supersonic flight on 12 October 1971. (*Aeroplane*)

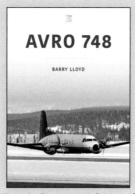
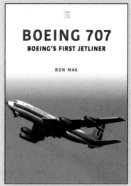